U1

MW01482072

Freedom from the Prison of Identity

From the Evolution-Directed Therapy Series
By Doug Bartholomew, MS, LMHC

Table of Contents

Un-Stuck

Freedom from the Prison of Identity

Spoon boy: Do not try and bend the spoon. That's impossible. Instead... only try to realize the truth.
Neo: What truth?
Spoon boy: There is no spoon.
Neo: There is no spoon?
Spoon boy: Then you'll see that it is not the spoon that bends, it is only yourself.

- The Matrix

INTRODUCTION

All of your limitations are imaginary!

Or, more specifically, the source of your limitations lies in your imagination, your paradigm, how you see the world and how you see yourself in the world. Once you realize that all you can change is your paradigm, all things become possible.

Because that is all you *need* to change.

*

There it is: that's the whole point. Once you understand this point many things will become easier for you. Until you do understand this point, many things will be much more difficult than they need to be.

This has been known for centuries, maybe millennia. This is the basis of many psychologies, most personal development literature, and is a part of many religions: every time we define ourselves or identify ourselves with something we immediately become limited to that definition or identity.

We limit ourselves when we identify with:

- Our intelligence or aptitudes.
- Our circumstances.
- How we think life works.
- What people expect of us.
- Things that have happened to us.
- Our role in our families or community.
- Our expectations.

It is your definition of who you are, your paradigm, which limits you. Which imprisons you. Once you understand this, really understand it, you are free to re-define yourself any way you wish and thereby become free to be the person you need to be, want to be.

Once you know that you are imprisoned in a prison of your own making, a prison of ideas, then you can make it go away; it disappears, and you can walk out. It will no longer be there. It really never was.

"It is not the spoon that bends, it is only yourself."

4

The purpose of this book is to help you understand:

- How your definition of who you are, your paradigm or identity, works; what its purpose or function is.
- How it imprisons you.
- Where it comes from.
- What your paradigm or identity currently consists of.
- Ways to dis-identify with your identity and paradigm so that you can let it go, build on it, and become who you need to be and want to be: an unlimited person.
- BUT MOST OF ALL TO KNOW THAT **YOU ARE NOT YOUR IDENTITY, YOU ARE NOT YOUR PARADIGM.** YOU ARE THE ONE THAT IS MAKING USE OF THOSE TOOLS, BUT YOU ARE NOT THOSE TOOLS.

Stephanie[1] was a perfect daughter to a perfect mother and a perfect father. They lived in a perfect home in a perfect town. She went to a perfect college and got perfect grades and married a perfect man.

Well, actually her parents were not that perfect. Okay, they were completely self- absorbed, flaming alcoholics who abused and neglected their children, but one doesn't talk about that. That would be imperfect and ungrateful.

And her husband wasn't actually all that perfect. Like her parents he was completely self-absorbed, but at least not an alcoholic. He had different addictions. But one doesn't talk about that. That would be ungrateful. That would be imperfect.

She was a perfect wife and perfect mother. She kept a perfect home and raised perfect children.

But that required that she continue to believe that this was the real her. She had to believe that this was all she wanted, that this was all she could do. She watched other women who were

---

[1] The examples I use of clients or other acquaintances are based on real people or combinations of real people, but the details have been modified to protect their privacy and confidentiality. Any resemblance to actual people is purely coincidental.

neither smarter nor better educated than she was, have more fulfilling lives. She had to believe that the life and marriage she had were the best she was capable of having, or she wouldn't be able to stay in that life.

One day a friend came to visit and noticed the work table in the home office was covered with papers.

"That looks important. What are you up to?" her friend asked.

Stephanie explained that in the process of doing the family taxes she realized that she could refinance the house at a lower rate and still pull out enough money to pay off all their debt and invest more in various parts of their portfolio, which she was also managing.

"Wow, I guess everyone is right," her friend said. "You really are some kind of stock broker."

"What?"

"Well, you are so good at everything, especially things that have to do with business and finance. We all figured you must have been some sort of finance person before you had kids."

Stephanie said the rest of that day she was in a fog. This didn't make sense but it did make sense. The only way she could justify her life was to believe that she couldn't make it in the world of business.

But what if she could?

This began an adventure of discovering who she really was, of debunking myths about limitations she didn't actually have.

In the end she had a fruitful, successful career and personal life. Her marriage didn't last but she found immense fulfillment – as well as terror and uncertainty – in a life based upon the reality of who she was, and not her old paradigm, her old limited and limiting ideas about who she was.

CHAPTER ONE

IDENTITY

"You are the driver, not the car."
-   Deepak Chopra

I need to help you understand what these terms and concepts are in order for them to make sense and in order for you to be able use them well. A concept is a mental tool, and when you have the right tools for the job the job goes more easily.

Identity is defined as everything we know about ourselves, the things which we feel define us and distinguish us from others.

Thus there are four parts to this discussion;

1.   Why we need an identity.
2.   The traits, qualities, and characteristics with which we identify.
3.   The external things, people, groups, ideas, causes, etc., with which we identify or feel connection.
4.   The rules, roles, and expectations which form our ideas of how things should work.

1. Why we need an identity

An identity is how we navigate that area between the chaos of not knowing who we are and having rigid identities which prevent us from adapting and learning and growing.

Dan Siegel describes the flow of our lives and consciousness as being like a river between two banks, rigidity and chaos[2].

---

[2] Siegel, Dan, *Mindsight; the New Science of Personal Transformation*

I envision it as looking something like this, constantly careening too close to one side or the other and then correcting our paths to come back to the middle:

CHAOS

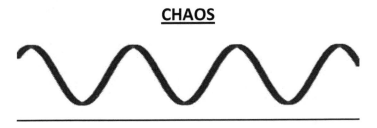

RIGIDITY

We have to have an identity in order to get through the day efficiently and comfortably. It is a practicality, a necessity. But it's not who I am any more than I **am** my driver's license or my address. We **need** a driver's license, a social security number, and an address. But that isn't who we **are**.

If, every morning when I got up, I had to re-decide if I was male or female, gay or straight, what my personality was, whether or not I had a job, what job I had, whether or not I went to work, what my relationship consisted of, I would never get anything done!

That would be chaos. I have to have some kind of consistent definition of myself just to get through the day.

However too much consistency can become rigidity and prevent adaptation and growth and learning. If I identify too much with my identity I won't be able to adapt to changing needs and changing situations.

My wife and I were at a street fair last spring. A man who looked at least in his fifties, if not older, was playing an electric guitar and singing. He had a little amp and a laptop which played the other parts of the songs playing in the background as he whipped out the riffs to old acid rock songs. He had long black hair, dark glasses, a snake skin vest, skin tight black pants and boots.

He had all the right moves. For a much younger person in a different time.

The guitar case was open at his feet for donations.

He didn't seem to notice the fifty years since those songs were popular, didn't even seem to notice that no one noticed him.

I bet there was a time when he really was cool. When it was working for him. But that time was long gone.

*

When the kids were little we had a family friend everyone liked. He was talented, engaging, and knew a little bit of everything. He was my age at the time, early forties. He'd had his teaching certificate at one time, but left teaching to have his own camera shop and photography studio. Somewhere in there he was selling real estate and being a pharmaceutical representative. I think he had a farm for a while. When we knew him he was a general contractor but was considering a move to software engineering.

In the middle of the chaos his family suffered, everyone was a nervous wreck and last I heard they'd all gone their separate ways.

So we spend our lives trying to live in that space between **too little** consistency – chaos – and **too much** consistency – rigidity.

We need just the right amount of identity to have consistency in our lives, but to not take it too seriously, in order to be flexible enough to adapt and survive.

Veronica considered herself to be a very moral person. In her profession she had to make many hard choices and she prided herself on always making the morally correct choice, even if it wasn't the easiest choice.

Her aunt, a well to do woman who had never married nor had children, made her the executor of her will. Veronica was biologically her closest living relative and thus, if there hadn't been a will, she would have been due to get the entire estate. However, Veronica had a copy of her will leaving all her money to some relatives who were distant biologically but to whom she was very close and needed the money desperately.

The story got interesting when, after the aunt died, Veronica learned that the will had never been filed and she had the only copy. She was faced with the painful moral dilemma that she could do the right thing, which would be to execute her aunt's will as written, or keep the money and no one would be the wiser.

Her husband was adamant that she didn't have to disclose the existence of the will. She could legally, he argued, simply leave all the money to the two of them!

Even though it caused a lot of stress in her marriage, she was clear that she wouldn't steal the money from the intended recipients, even though she could have hidden it.

She told me she never regretted the choice, nor the price she paid for making the right choice.

"That's just how I am!" she announced proudly. "I didn't have to think about it for even a second. That is how I do things!"

We have to understand that consistency, while helpful and comfortable, isn't reality. It is just a convenience. It's a tool, it's not who you are. If we think our identity is reality we will stop being flexible and adaptive to new circumstances. We run the risk of becoming rigid and non-adaptive. We will stop responding to our needs and limit ourselves to perpetuating that identity, even at the expense of our happiness.

And that is, in fact, what tends to happen quite often, and it causes a lot of unnecessary suffering. The rigidity and inflexibility which prevents us from being able to adapt and grow and change. The misery of not being someone you aren't anymore or never were.

Ted had been a very successful businessman before the crash. He belonged to the right club, lived in the right neighborhood and drove the right car. When the crash came he never recovered. He still clung to the identity that he was wealthy, that he could accomplish anything, and that he was part of the ruling class.

His idea of positive thinking was to deny reality.

He perseverated in spending at a level he could no longer afford and tried to keep living in a neighborhood of affluent people. He eventually had a mental breakdown when, after failing to adapt, they towed his car and foreclosed on his home.

*

Tom, on the other hand had grown up poor. No matter how much he succeeded he couldn't believe it. He couldn't identify with his new success. He became increasingly anxious about losing everything because he couldn't believe that he had it. The more money he made, the more he was afraid he'd lose it because he identified with his earlier poverty. He began to see problems when there were none. He began to perceive evidence that his wife was going to leave him or that his partners were going to steal his money, even though neither was true. He hid money and became a hoarder.

That is how we end up in a prison of our paradigm, our identity, and it can be hard to escape. Until we realize that it is a tool, it isn't who we are.

Some occupations, such as being a doctor, or being a minister, can become so integral to a person's identity that it is hard, if not impossible, to let go of that identity or allow it to change. I have known several people who were ministers at one point in their lives. The process of change can be painful to watch.

> **_Robert_** was a devout, impassioned minister. It was all he'd ever wanted to be. However he was also concerned about social causes. In fact, he believed they were one and the same. He kept directing his church toward ministering to the poor and the needy, which didn't work very well because he was in an affluent community which didn't really care about those things to begin with and, as time went on, the demographics grew more extreme, more affluent, and more unconcerned with the poor.
>
> He couldn't let go of his passion, nor could he adapt by going to a church or community which agreed with his passions. For him, that would be cowardliness, giving up, giving in.
>
> The congregation got smaller and smaller as fewer and fewer of the local people agreed with him. He still wouldn't adapt.
>
> His wife realized that what he really was a social worker in his heart, more than a minister, but the transition could nearly kill him. So he still didn't adapt.
>
> He stayed with his church until they had to close the doors. He blamed himself for the failure, he hated himself. He flailed around for several years working in various charities before he stopped calling himself "a pastor without a church" and simply got his degree in social work and began formally working as a social worker and met his spiritual needs by being a member of a church which agreed with him.

It took him almost twenty years and a lot of pain to adapt to the reality of who he was in the world in which he lived.

In the end, by finally adapting, he was able to do what he believed in and live like he wanted to live.

***James**, on the other hand, was more flexible. A truly good person, his goal was to bring more peace and happiness to the world. At first he was a minister like his father, but became disenchanted with the profession. He felt that only a fraction of his efforts went to the cause of peace.*

So he got his MSW after only a few years as a minister. He made a smooth transition into social work until, in the 1980's, that field almost vanished.

So then he combined his skills as a social worker and as a minister and became a therapist for ten or fifteen years. The last I heard he'd let go of that role and had become a teacher of sorts running a retreat center for people seeking peace.

By identifying with his cause, not his role, he was able to adapt more flexibly.

2. The traits, qualities, and characteristics with which we identify.

Each of us has hundreds, maybe thousands of traits, attributes and skills by which we can define or describe us, yet we choose only a few of them to consider our identity or who we are. And not necessarily the best or most accurate or most current at that!

- I am a farmer (not to mention my passion for remote controlled airplanes)
- I am a cook (not to mention carpentry)
- I am faithful (not to mention my passion for rock and roll)

In fact, most of the time we base our identity on outdated information and experiences. Simply a model of who we are which was useful to earlier circumstances, but not where we are now.

- We identify with or cling to our childhood or early upbringing.
- We identify with our college persona or beliefs or values.
- We identify with the peer group with which we identified at crucial times in our lives, such as being in the military or being together when we were inventing great things or accumulating wealth.
- We identify with how our bodies looked at specific times in our lives.

After a very unremarkable childhood, Chuck had gotten a basketball scholarship to a community college. His second year he was good enough that, for most of the season, he was being scouted by the scouts from several good four-year colleges. However, he tore his shoulder and couldn't finish the season and wasn't scouted any more. He didn't even complete his last quarter for his AA.

For the next thirty years any time he had a few too many drinks he'd tell the whole story as if it was yesterday. It was the only thing in his life which he felt identified him; the time he was a basketball star. Nothing else in his life – his wife, children, and adult career – ever came up because he was defined by his basketball career!

It was almost as if, having achieved that status, he didn't have to try any more, he didn't have to achieve anything else or grow or change, because he certainly didn't!

*

Marcy had failed at several jobs in her chosen career and was terribly depressed. This was her career! This was her plan! If she failed at this she failed at everything! What else could she do?

As we worked on grief and self-esteem issues, almost as an aside I sent her to the local technical college because they have a very good career guidance program which includes extensive testing.

She saved up the fee and came back two or three weeks later terribly excited. Bubbling with excitement!

"I found out that I have skills in areas I've never even thought of!" she exclaimed.

Her technical skills and aptitudes were at best average, but at everything interpersonal she excelled. Of all the career paths she had available, that she had both skills and aptitudes for, the most interesting was Project Management.

"I always knew I liked team work and team projects. It never occurred to me that I could make a career of it. I never visualized myself in that sort of job, that sort of role."

She quit therapy and enrolled in a training program leading to a certification in Project Management.

It can be useful to write down a list of all of the things with which you identify - the traits, skills, or attributes which you consider to be you:

I am _____.

I am _____.

I am _____.

I am _____.

I am _____.

I am _____.

Use as many pieces of paper as you need to make sure you list all of the things which make up your identity.

Now repeat the exercise but this time with other traits and attributes you left out. Things that you are or do with which you don't identify or include in your identity.

I could be _____.

I could be _____.

I could be _____.

I could be _____.

Again, use more pages if you need to.

What does this tell you? What can you derive from what you left out? Be a detective of *you*. Investigate *yourself* as if you were a mystery to be solved.

I did this one time with a woman who didn't list a single physical attribute as being part of her identity! She had no sense of herself as a physical being. She found the second half of the exercise threatening, but finally she wrote down "tall," and with a little more effort "athletic." Eventually she got up some steam and she went on and listed more and more traits that were her, but with which she hadn't identified:

Strong.

Competitive.
Fun loving.
Dancing.
Energetic.

She was quite excited to discover that she had a whole part of her life that she could have identified with but had never thought about. She had imprisoned herself in a very limited definition of who she was. However, by discovering this, she was able to open up a whole range of activities, pursuits, even a whole lifestyle change, to encompass and allow the identity she'd never allowed herself.

*

I did a similar exercise with a man who had very poor self-esteem, who felt like he'd never been accepted or liked by anyone in the world.

The first time through the list he identified with all the times he'd been rejected and ignored.

The second time through was hard, but he eventually began remembering birthday parties, times spent hanging out with friends, girls who'd approached him, and many more experiences he'd failed to identify with at first. As with most people in this situation, he at first objected that those other events were nice but not representative of who he was. However in time he became convinced that he'd based his identity on "probably 20% of my life, not the whole thing."

His first paradigm, the 20%, was his prison. By looking at the other 80% he challenged his old identity and allowed himself a larger, more satisfying identity.

So learn what you identify with and what you are leaving out. What the things are which you consider to be you, and which you *could* identify as being who you are.

<u>3. The external things, people, groups, ideas, causes, etc., with which we identify or feel connection.</u>

Humans are probably the most poorly designed animals on the planet. We can barely exist. In fact, without our connection with others of our own kind we **wouldn't** exist. We are only able to survive as a group because alone we are too vulnerable. This need to connect and identify is wired deeply into every cell of our nervous system, every cell in our bodies. Every aspect of our societies and culture.

Even at the anatomical level we crave connection with:

- A mate
- A family
- A clan or group or extended family
- A race
- An ethnic group
- A religion
- A social group
- A nation
- A cause
- Any variable or feature which we can hold in common.

One weekend my wife and I went to a medieval fair. I was impressed by the camaraderie and mutual support these people had for each other. They *belonged* and they were proud of that connection. It gave them connection and comfort and meaning and identity.

The next day we went to an antique show in another city. I noticed that there was a Civil War re-enactment group. They dressed the same as each other, shared the same interests and laughed and talked about the Civil War. They belonged and they were proud of that connection. Again, it gave them meaning and connection and identity.

There was another booth staffed by a rescue group which rehabilitated rescued parrots. Again I saw a level of connection and commitment between these people which was really the same as the people in the church in which I'd grown up, various support groups I've known, and most political parties. They had something they could identify with.

Even the kid in an AC/DC tee shirt was proclaiming "this is who I am! I am one of these people! I belong!" The people with the Christian fish symbols on their cars, bumper stickers that announce their political preferences, were all identifying themselves.

Part of knowing who we are is knowing what we identify with so that we can make conscious decisions about that identification.

One time a couple came in for therapy. The first thing I noticed was that he had a ring on with the logo "ES335". It was a subtle statement of who he was and what he believed, what he identified with.

"You have great taste in guitars," I commented.

He beamed. I'd noticed! We had a bond. His wife looked at me like I was some kind of idiot. She didn't understand the significance of the issue. She resented it. In fact, that was one of their marital issues. He felt that she didn't accept him for who he was and what he stood for.

But there was another side to it.

She was also making a statement about who she was and what she identified with by her appearance, how she dressed and acted. She'd made herself a living statement of a very different identification, a very specific person at a very specific time and place and age.

"This is who I am!" her appearance shouted just as clearly as his 409 ring shouted who he was. She felt just as unseen and unheard by him as he felt unseen and unheard by her.

And neither was aware of it so neither of them could make conscious, informed decisions about it.

*

The need for this connection is so great that people will actually act in ways which are not in their best interest rather than lose their connection with something outside of themselves. We see extreme examples in the cults where people will commit suicide rather than lose their connection with the group.

But more everyday examples are just as startling. Even the relatively bland "mainstream" religions and denominations can put their members in a position where they have to act against their own best interests, the best interests of their children, to adhere to the political or economic ideas of their group. People will make bad economic decisions in order to stay loyal to their political group. In many cases the drive to be connected to a group larger than themselves can motivate people to leave their marriages or give up their children.

This is certainly a prison of identity. In order to preserve that part of your identity you have to do things you don't really want to do, which aren't in your own best interests or those of your loved ones. All in the name of belonging.

In the mid 1970's when I was working in Chehalis, Washington, I encountered a case where a man belonged to a religious group which didn't believe in using medical intervention. His grandparents and parents and all his relatives and friends belonged to the group.

His one-year-old son had a serious stomach problem which could be easily cured with medicine, but could prove fatal if the child wasn't treated. His religious group said that he had to do without treatment in order to be part of their group.

In the end he had to file for legal separation from his wife, which also violated the rules of their group, file for custody of their son, leave his religious group and give up all of his friends in order to legally be able to get medical treatment for his son.

It nearly killed him. His grief was inconsolable. Without the group with which he'd identified his whole life he couldn't function, even though he'd saved his son's life. He'd lost almost everything he identified with and was hopelessly isolated.

His connection to his religion was so great that he couldn't adapt.

*

As late as 1974 various Japanese soldiers were still guarding islands in the Pacific Ocean, not accepting that the war was over, fighting on because of their deep commitment to the Imperial Japanese Army and the Emperor of Japan. This belief, this commitment to the thing that was larger than them – the empire, the army, the nation – was so implicit in their beliefs, their experience of the world, that they fought on without any support or contact with their homeland for up to 30 years.

I remember one was found in the 1960s and, when the interviewer asked him if he'd felt lonely or abandoned he looked at the interviewer with surprise and said "Why would I feel alone? I'm part of the Imperial Japanese Army!"

But they couldn't adapt. They could live for decades under circumstances that would kill most people. That's good. But they couldn't adapt or question those beliefs. That could be seen as not so good. They couldn't accept that the war was over and they couldn't go home to their families.

To illustrate this point, in the first column, list all of the things with which you identify, upon which you have built your identity. This can be something as large as a faith, a family, an ethnic group or political group, or as simple as a neighborhood, a group of friends, a musical group, an art style or a hobby.

Then, in the second column, write down the benefits of that connection, that belief.

Then, in the third column, write down the things that connection keeps you from being able to do, the ways it keeps you from being able to grown, change or adapt.

The connection, the beliefs, the groups, etc.	The positive things that identification brings you	The drawbacks, or inhibitions that come with that identification
_____	_____	_____
_____	_____	_____
_____	_____	_____
_____	_____	_____
_____	_____	_____
_____	_____	_____
_____	_____	_____
_____	_____	_____
_____	_____	_____
_____	_____	_____
_____	_____	_____
_____	_____	_____
_____	_____	_____
_____	_____	_____
_____	_____	_____

Use more pages as needed.

This is intended to make several points.

The first is, what does this tell you about who you are and what you connect with? Can you see the strengths and weaknesses this entails? There have been various times in my life where I've had to choose between clinging to the things to which I had identified, the affiliations I was identifying with, and my own ability to function as a human being. I had to go through this process of weighing out my continuity with the past identity and growing into the new one.

So in this regard, can you see that the identifications you have are purposeful, that those identifications are practical and give you certain benefits. This emphasizes that who you are is not determined by something external, but a choice we make, a choice for a purpose.

Knowing that we are making a choice makes the making of that choice more informed, more deliberate.

This is never a simple or painless process. Often there is a lot of grief which comes with letting go of old associations and connections.

That is where the second point comes in: that identification comes with a cost. It limits us and prevents us from being able to do other things. In order to make any informed choice we must know the price we are paying.

We pay a price for staying the same and we pay a price for moving on. There is always a price.

But that is what it means to grow and change. Letting go is the price we pay for moving forward.

4. The rules and roles we govern our own behavior and expectations with

What is our personality if not a collection of policy statements about what we do and don't do, what we do if "x" happens or if "y" happens? I love the stories about naturalists who will observe animals, bees, ants, almost anything and extrapolate the algorithms which describe their behaviors, their personalities, and can do so with great accuracy.

Are we that much different?

Most people who know me know that I have a deeply entrenched policy that if you give me a good opening line I will inevitably take it. I love puns and word games. Did I mention trivia?

- I will always take a chance to make a word joke.
- I will always take a chance to use a metaphor or allegory.
- I will always choose delta blues or classic rock over other forms of music.
- I am more likely to choose food based on its texture than on its smell.

Most of us, I think, take a lot of pride in the things we won't do. So there is a list or algorithm of what I won't do.

- I won't knowingly hurt someone's feelings.
- I won't knowingly make a joke at someone's expense unless I'm sure they will also think it is funny.
- I won't give in to blackmail.

Unfortunately, although we take pride in what we won't do, sometimes that is not accurate. It might merely be a vanity, comforting ourselves into believing that we are better than we are. The famous series of experiments by Stanley Milgram in the 1960s and 1970s and subsequent research has shown that this idea of what we won't do is more comforting than real.

Although we may like to think of ourselves as the sort of people who won't do X or Y or Z, the experiences and thousands of replications show that very, very few people, no matter how highly they think of themselves, won't eventually do what, in the course of the experiment, they have been led to believe is great cruelty and even murder, under the right circumstances.

So these ideas of what we will and won't do, who we are and who we aren't, provides another example of that space between chaos and rigidity which allows us the continuity we need to survive but the flexibility we need to adapt. They are nice ideas which keep us in the middle of the river, but they are only that, ideas. They aren't real. They are tools, and we need to know that in order to adapt and grow flexibly.

*

We also identify with the rules we apply to other people and often take great pride in the rules we require of others. Many religious groups consist almost entirely of the rules they require people to follow. Many such groups attain greater status by having greater expectations of other people.

Fairness is just another name for those rules we identify with. When people behave unfairly – by not following the rules any particular group considers "right" – we can react with great anger, even rage. Without the rules, we are afraid our worlds won't work. So, if we identify with these rules, someone breaking those rules threatens the very foundation of our existence. Our psychological survival.

Many years ago a friend of mine said a neighbor of his had driven home in the snow after a staff Christmas party, absolutely hammered. He managed to lose control of his car in the snow a few hundred feet from his own house and run the car into a telephone pole. He left it there and walked the few hundred feet home in the snow. Arriving home he immediately got into a nice, warm shower.

Moments later the police arrived. They'd been called by the person in front of whose home he'd cracked the car up. They simply followed the tracks to his door and arrested him for drunk driving.

The argument, the dilemma, is that my friend said they hadn't caught him while driving drunk so he was, literally, "home free" and the police were wrong to have arrested him.

My position, which I never should have mentioned, is that he had been, in fact, driving drunk and the charge was accurate.

Clearly my friend and I had very different sets of rules and each of us took pride in our separate lists of rules. In the rest of his life as well, the idea that if you can get away with something it's okay, was reflected in many of his decisions and, in fact, most of his disappointments.

And to be honest, my idealistic paradigm was equally naïve and inaccurate and accounts for many of my poor decisions and most of my disappointments.

*

A few years after that I had become a department manager at the mental health center and was then in on the management level discussions about staffing and planning. I was horrified to learn that my paradigm - that my job was to provide value to my employer and I would be rewarded by having a secure position – was completely wrong.

Instead the director and clinical director and business manager talked openly at those meetings about encouraging more turn over in staff so that they would only have to pay entry level wages! This was the opposite of what I believed! It meant that the longer I was there, the better quality work I did, I was actually working myself out of a job!

The business manager, a much wiser, more patient man, explained that "my job is to keep the doors open and I can't do that if I have a staff of long term senior employees getting paid higher wages."

I was outraged by this idea and took the self-righteous position that I would never do something like that. However, I also *wasn't running a business. It's easy for all of us to say "I would **never** do something like that!" when we aren't in that situation. It's an easy way to purchase self-esteem and pride.*

When I realized my idea of what the rules were had nothing to do with what the real rules of the mental health center were, at first I was angry. Then I made my plans to go into private practice and not judge the business strategies of the mental health center.

So if we are to learn who we are and what the prison of our identities are we have to ask, what are the rules with which you identify yourself?

What I will always do _____.

_____.

_____.

What I will never do_____.

_____.

_____.

What I will always expect from others _____.

_____.

_____.

Now ask yourself what is it that each of these rules, these beliefs, supports in your identity? What do they allow you to think or feel about yourself? In the book *Catch-22,* the author, Joseph Heller, in writing about a fictitious air base in WWII, describes a situation in which people purchased greater status by requiring stricter loyalty oaths (anti-communist statements required in the 1940s through the 1960s) in their departments than the other departments. The result was that the base became paralyzed.

In a similar manner, in the church in which I grew up, piety was in many ways, measured by the rigidity of the rules, the extremity of the rules, which one required of themselves and others. Several political groups I've worked with over the years showed the same phenomena; one purchased self-esteem and status by having increasingly extreme expectations and rules.

I'm not proposing that you give up the rules by which you live. Only that you become conscious of them and honest about the function or purpose they serve. Until you know you are doing it, you become the prisoner of those beliefs, those rules. Once you know you are choosing these beliefs and rules and values, and choosing them for practical reasons, you are in the position to make good decisions about them.

And, by owning those beliefs you are less likely to inflict them on others.

SUMMARY

We need to have an identity in order to have continuity in our lives.

Our identity provides us a way to stay in that zone between chaos and rigidity, but we can only stay there if we are aware of the way we identify with the components of our identity and the purpose they serve. If we have too little identity our lives become chaotic, but if we become too rigid we lose the ability to adapt and grow.

Our identity consists of:

1. The traits or aspects of ourselves with which we identify or distinguish ourselves from others.
2. The external things, such as groups, possessions, roles, or beliefs with which we identify or associate.
3. The rules or beliefs we have about how we should operate and expect others to operate.

CHAPTER TWO

Paradigm

In order to understand our identities we need to understand some of the ways our brains work, how we perceive the world and interact with it. In order to do so, we need to understand the concept of a paradigm, since we tend to think and understand things in terms of paradigms.

*

A paradigm is a very useful idea. It is a mathematical concept which has found a very practical role in the psychology of people and how they interact. It takes the elements we put into our identity and adds the concept of the rules, rituals, and protocols which run our lives.

I find it very useful for helping me understand the huge volume of information which makes a person a person. Both myself and others.

*

The simple definition is that a paradigm is:

1. A defined set of objects, and,
2. The rules by which they interact.

Chess, for example, is a set of objects – the board, the chess pieces and the two people playing the game – and the rules by which they interact, the rules for the game. As long as people follow the rules it can be a very orderly, productive experience. If someone violates the rules, such as jumping up, punching the other person in the face, then it isn't orderly, it isn't chess any more.

I have two friends who are professional MMA fighters, but the idea is the same. The paradigm consists of a ring, the equipment, two fighters, and the rules by which they fight. It is a different paradigm than chess, but, like chess, if people are operating in terms of the same paradigm, it is an orderly experience.

In this case punching the other person in the face is perfectly normal but if you ask for time to think you will probably get hit. What works or doesn't work depends on the game at hand. What is right or wrong depends on the paradigm.

*

The strategies we follow in dealing with a cold, fixing our cars, and paying our bills are all governed by the paradigm we are using. And our success at dealing with those things is limited by the paradigm we are using. The housing/stock market crisis in the mid 2000's was, in many people's minds, including Alan Greenspan, a failure of their paradigm. He admitted that, based upon what happened in those days "I've learned that some of my fundamental assumptions about free market corrections were wrong". He, like everyone else, had a paradigm – a list of the variables and elements and the rules by which they interact – and in this case he needed to have a different paradigm in order to make more successful decisions.

There was a paradigm for how the solar system worked. The sun and moon and stars rotated around the earth. Then Galileo and Copernicus came up with a new paradigm; that the moon circled the earth and the rest of the solar system rotated around the sun. It made more sense and made astronomy much easier. However, since it challenged the status quo, it was met with great resistance.

All of our successes and failures are the success or failure of the paradigm we are using, in any aspect of our lives. Learning is a process of learning new paradigms, change and personal development is a process of moving from a small paradigm to a large paradigm.

Identity as a part of our paradigm

As I discussed in the previous chapter, our identities are a paradigm.

For example we always pick a finite number of elements to define ourselves. Most of us define ourselves *by a very small fraction of the real data about who we are and the world in which we operate*. Of the thousands of things which might interest us, we pick only a few. Of all of the thousands of traits or skills or attributes we could pick, we identify with only a few. The entire Human Potential Movement of a few decades back was based on this simple idea, that there is more of you which you aren't using than there is that you are aware of. By tapping into that unknown territory you can increase your personal resources algebraically.

Walter was seriously depressed. He felt he had failed at everything.

Actually, he had failed at two things; he'd failed as a professional baseball player in his early 20's and in his late 30's he'd failed as a small business owner.

He also felt that "everyone" believed he was an idiot, a failure.

However as we discussed it further there were dozens of things at which he'd succeeded for each thing he'd failed at. He was nearly a straight-A student in high school and college, he was liked by almost everyone, and he was a great father, a great husband, well-liked by their friends and neighbors. In between baseball and real estate he'd been a very successful high school teacher.

As we looked even deeper he was basing his idea that "everyone" thought he was an idiot on the opinions of only three people, none of whom he respected.

The conclusion we reached was that with the exception of baseball and real estate he was a very successful, respected, competent person.

We also discovered that he had a wide range of skills, traits, and assets which would help his career, all of which he'd ignored in perseverating on using only the skills that had worked in baseball, to the exclusion of all of his other skills.

Once he stepped out of the prison of his paradigm he was able to build a successful career on the skills he had previously ignored.

*

We also define who or what is in that paradigm, the elements in our world.

This can be the people in our world, such as family and friends and co-workers. But it also includes everyone we identify with, our reference group. That would be "rich people" or "poor people". It could be "nice people" or "not nice people". "People who like me" and "people who don't like me."

It also includes places. For me, my world consists of where I live, where I've been and places I go. When my boys were little I knew every comic book store and every baseball park in town. Now I don't. When I grew up I knew where every church in the neighborhood was, and who went there. Now I don't. At this phase of my life I know where every hardware store, every car parts store, and every book store is.

For me I see it as a map with places and people I identify with drawn large and every place else seen dimly at best.

And finally, ***the rules by which they interact.***

These are the rules, traditions, expectations, and rituals by which you interact with the people and events and circumstances in your life.

These constitute your role and the behaviors allowed you in this paradigm. In your world.

> *One day, when my oldest son was in high school and my youngest was in junior high school we went to visit my mother in her assisted living apartment. I helped her get her remote control on her TV working, fixed her phone and gave her a computer to use on the internet.*
>
> *When we were on our way home my oldest appeared angry, so I asked him what the problem was.*
>
> *"When you are around your mother you are young and limber and you can fix anything. But when you are around Nate and I you are old and stupid and can barely move and can't even figure out how to turn on your own TV!"*

He was right; around my children I'm old and around my mother I'm young!

Not only do we have rules about how we act around categories of people – for example around people who are older or younger than us, richer or poorer, smarter or less smart – but also specific groups, like around police, doctors, babies, pregnant women, people who don't signal left turns.

Even though we may not like to admit it, if we take the time to think about it, we all really do have a very elaborate and specific set of rules about how we interact with the people, places and things in our world. It will be different for each of us. But it's there. And unless and until we are aware of it we will follow that formula quite loyally.

So that is our world, our paradigm: everyone in our world, everything in our world, and the rules by which they interact.

How this relates to my growth and freedom

Many of the people I've worked with the last forty years have been people for whom their roles, the rules of their paradigm, were limiting them from doing what they needed to do, being who they needed to be. Who they needed to be. Usually it was a paradigm which worked for the time when it was created, but not since then.

Julie was raised by an ineffectual, passive father and a demanding, dependent, self-absorbed mother. From birth she was the caretaker for everyone, always putting her own needs last in order to prevent her mother from "wrecking everything". Her demeanor and presentation were blunt, harsh, and had a childlike concreteness. Her attitude toward her health, appearance, social life, and happiness was austere and self-denying.

Her harshness was fueled by something unseen; she had never been able to do anything she wanted, only what she had to do. Her social life as a young woman always put the family first. As an adult she appeared much older than her calendar age. She literally did not make a place for her own happiness in her life.

She thought she was the victim of her circumstances, when, in fact, she was only the victim of the role she had defined for herself. Her circumstances were such that she clearly had the opportunities and resources for a very happy, pleasurable life.

Her statements were very clear;

"I'm not the sort of person who is happy all the time."

"I'm the person everyone expects a lot from."

It wasn't her circumstances, it was her role, her definition of herself which imprisoned her.

Looking at our lives and our identities this way can make many things make more sense, especially our problems. We can only function within the paradigm, within the definitions and roles of our paradigm. We can't do anything which doesn't fit within our paradigm, our current list of behaviors and resources and ideas with which we identify, by which we define ourselves.

In other words, it is not the problem which makes a problem a problem, it is the paradigm with which we try to solve the problem. If the solution to the problem lies within our paradigm, we solve it, it's done, and we move on. We probably wouldn't even think that there was a problem in the first place.

But what if something is called for which lies outside of our paradigm? Then we can't solve it any more than a pre-Copernicus astronomer could predict the movements of the heavens, or a navigator who believed the Earth was flat could plot the shortest route from Hong Kong to Seattle.

Several years ago we were at a park with a group of friends. One woman had just gotten a new dog. It was a cool day, and she was only going to be there for a while, so she left the dog in the car and went over to pay her respects.

Unfortunately, she left her keys on the dashboard, and the dog, being just a puppy, jumped all over the car and hit the button which locked all of the doors.

No problem! One woman there was raised on a farm and I am an incurable tinkerer, so we immediately began the clothes hanger procedure. One of the other guests simply called AAA for a tow truck to come unlock the door.

My farmer friend and I both take great pride in our (dubious) abilities to fix nearly anything. My other friend took pride in his ability to pay for things. It never occurred to him to open the door, and it never occurred to my farmer friend and me to call anyone. In both cases we were limited to the behaviors in our paradigm.

By the way, she and I beat the AAA truck by fifteen minutes!

However our options, our and our friend's, were both limited to those things in which we took pride.

The point here is not that one approach or the other was better or worse. Each response was perfectly valid for the people involved. The point here is that each of us was limited to the responses in our paradigm. More flexibility could have resulted in less suffering had our "fix" failed.

There are countless examples in my personal life and professional life of suffering which is caused by our inability to operate outside of our perceived roles or paradigms.

Again, and this is one of the most important points of the book, it is not the problem which makes something a problem, it is the paradigm, the prison, which keeps us from adapting which makes the problem a problem.

For example, in order to adapt I have had to take an oath with my wife to never again try to fix a car. It costs too much in the long run to repair my repair jobs. Paying for car repairs used to be outside of my paradigm. I have expanded my paradigm with good results!

In that regard, I stepped outside of my paradigm into a larger one, I stepped outside of the prison of my paradigm and found myself free to respond in a new, more adaptive manner. One which freed me.

CONGRUENCE, CONSISTENCY AND CLINGING

Now, this is where it gets really interesting.

Whether we call it our paradigm or schema or ego or identity or any other name, it is our most important survival tool. As I've said several places our success or failure at anything, including or very survival, is determined by how accurate and effective our paradigm is.

- It's our map.
- It's our compass.
- It's our tool box.

Nature, being very survival oriented, has built in some pretty sophisticated defense mechanisms to protect this paradigm in order to protect our survival, to protect **us.**

Collectively these various defense mechanisms comprise all of the classic defense mechanisms, such as denial, displacement, repression, projection, etc. and the general umbrella term of resistance. It isn't a negative thing; it's designed to save your life!

Specifically, it's designed to save your life by protecting the tool kit by which you survive, with which you protect yourself. Every defense mechanism, and resistance itself, all, directly or directly serve to protect the status quo of the paradigm, primarily by **discounting disconfirming information.** Specifically, any information which would question the validity of your paradigm.

Wendell's story is a story about lying to oneself.

Wendell didn't quite make it in college, and didn't quite make it in any of the jobs he tried because he had trouble getting along with other employees and really didn't want to do what he was told. He didn't want to admit it but it was true.

He wanted to marry his girlfriend but she, realistically, didn't want to get married until he had a job. A career would be great, but she'd settle for a job.

Desperate to convince her that he was a better investment than he really was, he hit on a buddy who worked in a prosthetics lab. He didn't care one way or another about the work, but the more he learned about it the more he felt he could make a career out of it without working too hard. In those days you could make a good living at it without a whole lot of training.

He went for it and she married him.

At first it worked just fine. He grew his business and hired a few technicians and, for a while he believed that he had it made. For a while he convinced himself and his wife that he was a good businessman. He could keep up this growth forever, right? He was following all those formulas for success that were popular back then, right?

Gradually there were subtle changes in the technology which made it easier and easier to make low end prosthetics, and harder to make more sophisticated products, but he shrugged off the implications of those changes. He convinced himself that he was more than capable of overcoming those changes. He was slow to realize that he was paying a lot for craftsmen when, increasingly, simple technicians would do. At first he resisted the change. He liked his status and his role as a boss who bragged that "we don't do anything the cheap way."

The world disagreed.

By the time he couldn't ignore the changes any more he had to lay off all of his craftsmen and was forced to do all the work himself. He'd never liked the work and he didn't like learning new things. He liked making other people do it. He'd never admitted it before, but it was true.

Then came the computerized technology.

By this time his business was so far in the hole that he couldn't afford to buy the equipment to compete, and, even then, the profit margin wouldn't pay the bills. Actually, he wasn't paying *the bills. Rather than admit failure he began cutting corners, cheating on his book keeping, borrowing to pay debt.*

And then it all collapsed.

"I don't know what he was thinking!" his wife cried out. "He lied to me for years! Why didn't he just close the business and get a real job?"

"I lied to myself first," he mumbled in misery. "It was the only thing I knew how to do so I couldn't let myself see that it was all over."

He also realized that he was denying disconfirming information about his wife, his children and his marriage. And lying to them about who he was. Things were much worse at home than he'd let himself realize.

"If I was truthful about my marriage and my family I would have to be honest about who I was and I really didn't want to do that. I wanted to keep seeing myself the way I saw myself during the gravy days. But eventually it didn't matter."

After everything collapsed he had no choice but to see things realistically. He looked at his life and himself through more accurate eyes and in the process became more effective at things he did. He found a new career and started his life over at fifty. It was hard, but at least it was based on reality.

"It's weird," he said at the last session. "I'm less than half as successful as I was at the top of the market, but now that I'm honest with myself, I don't think I'm all that bad."

This force to distort reality to conform to our beliefs, our paradigm, is so great that it even has a name – cognitive dissonance – and decades of research to back it up. Our fear of losing our paradigm, our map and tool kit, is so great that we will even fail rather than change it.

As with most things in this book, and in the therapy I do, I prescribe consciousness as the first step in change. Consciousness and deliberateness.

When I do this as a workshop I encourage participants to write – or even scrawl! – their negative thoughts, their resistance, their disagreements all over the workbooks as they go. To become as conscious as possible of all the voices in their heads which are resisting change or freedom. When I do therapy with people most of the time I encourage clients to be as vocal as possible about their disagreements and resistance.

*"Keep your friends close
And your enemies closer."*

Sun Tsu. *The Art of War*

This is even more important in personal growth than in warfare. We have to be intimately conscious of our resistance, what is going on inside of ourselves which relates to change and growth, the resistance, the fear, the rationalizations.

By accepting resistance as a natural part of human interaction and growth, by giving it the dignity and respect it deserves, it stops being compulsive or unconscious. We bring it out into the open where it can be discussed. It becomes a valuable tool for expediting our growth and change.

Gary had been in one form of therapy or another off and on since he was ten. Sometimes it was very harmful. However, given his complex history, medical conditions and mental issues, to say nothing of personal and professional and financial issues, there wasn't much choice.

He struggled to live in a very tiny, proscribed, miserable way of living and relating in which the only things he wanted to do or needed to do caused such fear and emotional pain that he could do nothing.

He was a prisoner. In solitary. In a Gulag.

He was extremely guarded and often refused to participate in some part of the therapy or the other. I made a point of

41

encouraging him to resist as much as he needed to and that I understood it and that it made sense. Eventually it became almost a joke. He would laugh and tell me what an idiot I was, how nothing that we did could work, and so forth. And then we would do it. In time he was almost kind to his resistance, respectful of it. We spoke openly and articulately about it, without any sort of coarse "confrontation" or insistence that he change.

Each time we went through it he became more and more able to move beyond his old limitations, into a new paradigm. A new way of experiencing himself. A new way of understanding that experience of himself. He acknowledged his fear and pain about moving beyond everything he'd ever known. He acknowledged the survival value of it, the good intention behind it. And, feeling that fear and pain, moved on.

As of this writing his health is slowly improving, his work situation is going much, much better and his personal life is in the process of becoming more satisfying.

And at every point he verbalizes, even acts out, his resistance.

And I thank him for it.

This resistance takes many forms, which usually are described as congruence, consistency and clinging. They are very similar with some subtle but important differences.

Congruence. In this context, congruence relates to thinking and feeling and consistency is used to describe our behavior. Congruence is when we only let ourselves think and feel and believe things which don't challenge what we have always thought and felt and believed. Otherwise it might challenge that old paradigm. Which are incongruent with how we expect ourselves to think and feel, or to do so in ways incongruent with our former identity.

Any time you have said or thought or felt "I'm not that sort of person" you have been showing congruence with your old paradigm, your unwillingness to think outside of it. That isn't bad, when it works in your best interests, or makes your life more comfortable. It's only a problem when it prevents you from growing. You just need to see it for what it is and know that you are doing it.

Consistency is the behavioral equivalent. It's when your paradigm or personality or ego resists doing things which are different from what you have always done. To preserve the paradigm keeps your behavior within the paradigm.

I have seen numerous businesses, families and careers fall apart because someone chose consistency over adaptation. Doing what they'd always done, rather than what they needed to do.

Clinging is when we become attached to an issue, trait, belief, or anything else with which you identify and resist letting go of it. In meditation this specifically refers to clinging to feelings which are counter-productive and are standing in the way of growth and change. There was a case in the news a few years ago about a woman who'd had cancer previously which had since been cured and she was well. However she clung to that identity and continued to pose as a cancer victim and raised money for her treatment. In the TV article she was adamant that she was still a cancer victim, even in remission.

I've had several couples over the years where they came in for marital therapy ostensibly to resolve some issue. In one case it was infidelity, in a second case it was something he'd done without telling his wife, in a third it was an unexplained lie, and so forth. This is the daily fare of marital therapy.

However in some of the cases the offended party continued to feel offended long after the problem was dealt with.

- The affair had been five years earlier, he'd told his wife about it immediately and stopped it, had explained it, and made his amends, but she was still insistent that they needed to stay in therapy forever. She didn't want to reconcile yet, but didn't want to end the relationship. She was clinging to the issue long after it was no longer functional.

- In the second case both parties had been unfaithful, they both explained it and made their amends, but it was the husband who clung to the role of the cuckold. He accepted that she had made her amends, and had nothing else he was asking for, but, in his own words "I can't stop thinking of what she did." He was clinging; he wasn't letting go.

*

It is amazing how much power it gives us to become aware of our own resistance, the ways in which our paradigm or ego is protecting itself. When we are aware of that process and accept it and own it we can make much better choices, more conscious choices.

- "Oh, I know that feeling, it's resistance."
- "Oh, I know that feeling, it's clinging."
- "Oh, I see what I'm doing, I'm denying."

In the book "Feel the Fear and Do It Anyway, the author, Susan Jeffers, advises us that if we are never afraid it is because we are always staying in our comfort zone. That to truly be brave and growing we must keep pushing forward at a level with enough discomfort that we know we are pushing our limits, but not so much that we feel overwhelmed. Then and only then do we know we are going in the right direction.

If we aren't incurring some resistance, we are not growing. If we encounter too much resistance, we are going too fast and will probably give up. We have to know the feeling of pushing just hard enough, not too hard, not too little.

SUMMARY

1. A paradigm is a defined set of objects and the rules by which they interact.
2. Our identity is a paradigm in that it is a collection of everything by which we identify ourselves, all the things in our world, and the rules by which we interact with the world.
3. At any given Moment we are limited to what is within the paradigm, whether it is our definition, our behaviors, what we can do, or what we can comprehend or think about. This is what limits us.
4. Because our paradigm is crucial to our survival there are many mechanisms which are built into us which protect it, all of which boil down to various ways to deny disconfirming information and prevent us from looking or acting outside of the paradigm. This can be called resistance or defense mechanisms.
5. In order to grow and change and adapt we have to become intimately aware of that resistance, conscious of it and accept it and learn to use it as a resource.

CHAPTER THREE

What is a Problem?

There are no problems in nature. There are no dilemmas, no conundrums, no paradoxes or contradictions. None of those are real: they don't exist in nature. Nature just keeps doing what nature does.

Cause and effect, cause and effect, cause and effect. Birth, reproduction, death. Birth, reproduction, death.

Problems, as we know them, exist only in our heads. They are only the result of the limitations of how we see them. They represent and illustrate the flaws in our understanding of the world, the inadequacies of our paradigm.

Consider the lowly Duck Billed Platypus. Over a million generations of them have been born, lived, bred, had children, and died without knowing the problem they posed for human scientists. Or caring. They are furry, warm blooded animals who nurse their young, which makes them mammals, right? But they also have the bill of a duck, webbed feet and lay eggs, which makes them a duck, right? And they are venomous, which makes them a reptile, right?

It was never a problem for the Duck Billed Platypus, though. Because they just were. But for the scientists, for humans, it was a huge problem because it challenged their paradigm. Their way of seeing things in the world. They just didn't fit!

There are no problems, dilemmas, or paradoxes in nature. That is only a phenomena of the limitation of our paradigms. The Duck Billed Platypus, by not fitting into our paradigm, the way scientists explained nature, demonstrated a flaw in that system.

Eventually scientists changed the system by making a category just for the platypus. The world never changed, just the paradigm.

*

Given that so much of our lives is proscribed by the problems we face and that so much of our time is spent solving problems it is amazing that the research about what problems are has gotten so little attention.[3] Even a cursory understanding about how this works can reduce our frustration and make our lives easier. Especially once we understand that the problem isn't the problem, the paradigm which doesn't include the solution is the problem. That makes it much easier.

As a young man I struggled with trying to fix my cars until a friend of mine, later to become a famous scientist, explained that all I needed to know was fuel, compression and ignition. All problems with cars boil down to those three variables. After that it all made sense.

I will attempt a brief description of these ideas here, because our ideas about what problems are can be a huge part of imprisoning ourselves in a prison of our own making. Essentially, a firm understanding of this is like getting the key to the prison.

In this chapter we will discuss;

1. A problem is a solution which lies outside of our paradigm.
2. A problem is a solution which makes the problem worse. Solutions cause problems!
3. The only real solution is to change the paradigm.

---

[3] Watzlawick, Paul, Weakland, John, Fisch, Richard. *Change; Principles of Problem Formulation and Problem Solution.*

1. *A problem is simply a solution which lies outside of our existing paradigm. When you change your paradigm it isn't a problem anymore.*

We can solve any problem which needs a response which can be found in our existing skill set. That's not a problem. If I have a Phillips screwdriver I can take out Phillips head screws all day and twice on Sunday. But if I don't have that tool, if it lies outside my tool kit, I can't do anything.

Both personally and professionally I have not run into any exceptions.

For example I have been doing crisis calls, crisis outreach, suicide intervention, emergency talk-downs, and similar not-quite-your-everyday-day-at-work activities since 1974. While I take this very, very seriously, I have a large skill set for those situations. Not perfect, but large. I'll work hard in those situations but I will have a response.

That's not a problem, that's just work.

In the previous situation my friend did not have a response for getting into a locked car. I did.

So he couldn't respond. That would have been a problem if he didn't have someone he could call to get into the car. Calling people and paying them to do things is in his skill set, his paradigm, not mine. So he did it.

However, he is a gifted businessman, with a range of financial skills I can only guess at and admire. I have run into many situations I have struggled with, which, for him, would be no problem. A phone call.

What is difficult or easy depends on whether or not the response lies within our paradigm.

Everything you know how to do, which exists in your current paradigm

Potential solution

So the problem isn't the problem. The paradigm or belief system which doesn't include the solution is the problem.

Let me say this again; a problem is only a problem insofar as your definition of yourself, your paradigm, forbids you to access the solution, or precludes it.

Eddie went to college to run businesses. It was all that anyone in his family had ever done, all that he'd ever thought about. "My family and I talked about what was going on that day on Wall Street the way some families talked about sports or movies."

His family called people who weren't business people "Munchkins" and "Little People" or just "idiots." Everything he did, the way he was raised, the activities he pursued in school, were all designed for him to attain a superior place in society.

Right out of college he found himself working in a large corporation in which new employees and people lower on the totem pole were treated "as if I was one of the Little People!" He wanted more deference, more admiration than he was getting. That was how he'd always perceived himself. Superior.

His father advised him to shut up and play the game and get even later but he found it intolerable, it didn't fit into his identity, his life plan. He was enraged.

He married a trophy wife who would be good for his business image and bought a nice trophy house but not the mini mansion

he expected. He was so upset at the way he was treated at work that he eventually offended everyone and had to start over at another corporation, one slightly less prestigious.

Over the next ten years he lost one job after another, each one a more bitter pill to swallow, each one a step down which he found inexplicable. He lost the trophy wife, and she took the kids, but he kept the trophy house. He tried starting his own company, and failed, he started a small business and failed. Each time he became more and more angry, enraged, unable to comprehend what was wrong with the world that someone as qualified as himself was treated so badly. It had to be someone's fault. It had to be one or more really evil people. It had to be that the world was an evil place.

He was reduced to selling off his possessions and doing odd jobs to make his mortgage and child support payments.

When he realized he'd have to sell the house he became suicidal, detached from reality.

"I was upset about what I was losing, but what was really getting to me was being one of the Little People. For a while there I would rather die than be one of the Little People. What stopped me was the kids. I couldn't die and leave the kids with that memory of their Dad."

He did a good job upgrading the old house and selling it, and was able to pay off his debt and start a modest one man business.

"I was one of the Little People. We'd have lunch at the same Little People cafés and coffee shops. We'd have beers at the same Little People bars after work. Sometimes they would invite me over for dinner or barbecue. I bought a crappy Little People's house and I started having them over for dinner or barbecue. I learned how to get along. I had to learn how to not be so judgmental. I learned how to respect hard working people who were trying to feed their children. The people I used to ridicule."

51

In the next few years he reduced himself to just working hard and paying his bills and getting along with everyone. No one knew about his education, his past wealth, his past trophy wife. His failures.

As the years went by he got a reputation for being a person who did good work, who kept his word and treated people with respect. His business grew slowly but surely as he focused more on being a good businessman and less on being a rapacious member of the ruling class. He added a few employees, expanded his business, got a nice house and married a not-trophy wife.

The last time I saw him he was doing quite well, living far below his means and happily married.

At first his paradigm looked like this

The option of being modest and easy to get along with was simply not a part of his paradigm, not a part of his reality. A crucial part of his reality was that being superior was a sign of winning, a sign of "being there", so getting along was a sign of failure, not success. So he couldn't do it.

That made it a problem. The problem wasn't the problem, the paradigm which precluded success was the problem.

After a lot of hard knocks and soul searching his paradigm looked like this;

Being a part of the species

Being a good father

Getting along with others

A LARGER DEFINITION OF SELF

He created a larger definition of himself, of his identity or paradigm, in which getting along, not being arrogant and self-serving, was an option. It became automatic and part of who he was.

He explained that in the world in which he grew up and had spent most of his life if someone made a mistake you would jump on it and ridicule them. In the new world if he had his new friends over for barbecue and someone made a mistake or said something he disagreed with, he'd just let it be, and everyone got along.

Getting along was now an option, where it hadn't been before.

It wasn't a problem anymore. What once was impossible was now natural. He changed his paradigm to include the new behavior.

*

The exact opposite occurred in the case of Zelda.

Zelda's mother was fifteen when Zelda was born. They were very poor and lived in a bad part of town. Her Mom was a maid and cleaning lady and janitor in a cheap motel, and glad for the work. A small room, barely large enough for the two of them, came with the job. Compared to many of the other kids in town, she was doing okay.

So her Mom didn't want to rock the boat. Her strategy was simple; say yes to everyone, get along with everyone, and don't ask for any more than you are offered.

Zelda herself adopted that world view, that paradigm. In school she was quiet, never answered any questions, never volunteered for anything, and never joined anything. She didn't get good grades because she never tried; that was for the other kids, not for her. She didn't want to stand out or become visible.

Her crisis came in Junior High School.

Her school counselor said she wanted a meeting with Zelda and her mother, but couldn't call her because they had no phone in their tiny motel room. So the counselor wanted Zelda to bring her mother in for a parent/child consultation. However, when Zelda asked her mother, she was too afraid to come in.

This went back and forth for several days, and finally the school counselor just showed up at the motel after school and met with them in their motel room. She was horrified at the living conditions. They were meager. Not unclean: Mom was an impeccable house keeper. But it was meager to the point of deprived.

"I understand the problem more now," the counselor explained. "But we still have a problem. Zelda's test scores put her in the gifted level of ability, but her school performance has always

54

been just above failing. She isn't a behavior problem. She actually doesn't interact at all."

"However," she went on, "we are facing the problem that you aren't able to provide her with the support she needs in order to be able to make the most of her educational opportunities."

The way Zelda and her mother heard this was that if Zelda didn't start doing better in school she'd be taken away.

"I was so scared I just started doing better in school. It wasn't hard for me, because I had always not done well in spite of understanding the material. I just didn't want to be visible. So now I decided I had to be visible."

In one short year she went from invisible to very, very visible. She got almost straight A's with very little effort. Unfortunately, being visible meant she also became more popular, at least among the smart kids. The next year she was in the advanced classes instead of the remedial classes. She was with a whole different group of kids. Kids who hadn't known her before.

"It really scared me. I didn't know how to do things or handle things. All I knew was how to be nice to people and say yes to everything."

Her Mom wasn't able to afford school clothes for her, and she was too young to legally get a job, so the school counselor got her a work-study job at the library so she could at least look a little more like the other kids.

In short order she made new friends, got a boyfriend, and, because she still felt undeserving, unequal, she said yes to everything and, by the time she was sixteen, she was pregnant. She lost the boyfriend immediately, but kept the baby and she and her mother raised the baby in their tiny motel room. She stayed in school.

"I thought things were different, but they weren't. I may have been getting better grades but I was still invisible, I still didn't matter, I was just another statistic."

She went back to being invisible, not making eye contact, and not asking for much. But now she had one new asset: she realized she could get really, really good grades and could parlay that.

"I didn't apply for scholarships to any of the good colleges, after all, I had a two year old kid and I was poor. So I applied for scholarships to the crummy state colleges nearby. The ones who would take people like me."

She stayed invisible and unobtrusive in college and got an unremarkable teaching degree from an unremarkable state college. However, some of her college papers caught the attention of some of the professors who passed them on to other people.

She had inadvertently, and unconsciously, come to someone's attention.

Still living in great shame about her poverty and her early pregnancy she didn't ask for much and didn't get much. She just got by. She didn't date and, although she had many friends at school, she avoided a social life.

"By the time I got my job my son was old enough for kindergarten, so I moved into the catchment area for my school and he just went to school with me. It was perfect!"

And then the crisis came.

"It was just like when the school counselor showed up at the motel, only different."

The ideas she'd proffered in college, combined with her outstanding teaching ability and high test scores, had brought her to the attention of the very Ivy League colleges she had been avoiding.

She was being recruited into a think tank which would, incidentally, involve her being in a graduate program and getting a doctorate in education and very high pay while she was at it.

This was a huge crisis. "I didn't even think it was real. It was completely beyond anything I'd ever thought about myself. I was pretty sure they were just lying to me or making fun of me."

There were many more crises along the way but she had a good mentor and several good advisors who got her through the various adjustments to being in the upper crust of education in the U.S.

"They protected me and taught me how to do what I needed to do. They showed me how to dress and act, how to behave at high level cocktail parties, how to talk to famous people."

When I met her she had been running in the highest levels for some time. She was married to man she met politically, her son was in a good college and ostensibly her past was behind her.

She was in the fight for her life, professionally. She had long ago moved past her mentors and advisors. She was working on something she believed in with all of her heart, with every fiber of her being but she'd have to go to the mat for it. She'd have to fight for it every inch of the way.

She'd have to take the gloves off and stop being nice.

"This is way beyond just asking for what I wanted. I've never asked for what I wanted. I was just grateful for what I was given. Now it matters, now I'm not willing to be nice or passive or accepting. Now I'm going to have to pull out all the stops. I'm going to have to fight dirty with no option to fail. This is the real thing! And I don't know how!"

*

This is the exact opposite of the task for Eddie. For him, demanding what he needed and wanted, going the distance for what he believed in, was something he'd learned in the crib. Getting along was outside of his paradigm. In Zelda's case it was the opposite. Believing in herself, asking for what she wanted, going the distance to get what she needed, was what was outside of her paradigm. Outside of her identity. Getting along was all that she knew.

Her paradigm shifts would look something like this;

In each of her crises the response she needed was outside of her paradigm, so instead of just trying harder, each time she expanded her paradigm to include what she needed to do.

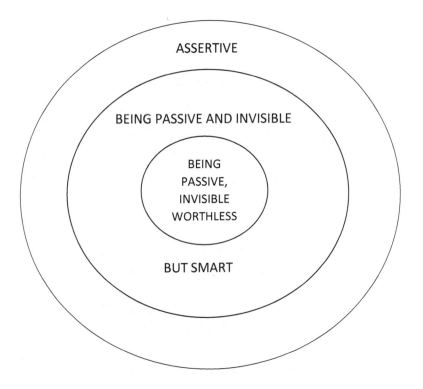

2. A problem is a solution which makes the problem worse. Solutions cause problems.

My first real job was in the tiny town of Chehalis, Washington, in 1975. As I approached town I-5 became a causeway with water in every direction. I didn't know it then, but the area flooded often. I remember a feedlot on the West side of the freeway with a large sign reading "Flood Control is Mind Control!" with a dead cow floating in front of the sign.

It came up in conversation when I talked to the office manager, who had grown up there. She explained that I-5 had only been built ten years earlier and at the time there was a controversy about it. The locals knew that the river flooded periodically, and the freeway was being built in a flood plain. They tried to convince the highway people to build it ten feet higher to accommodate the floods.

They lost.

It was cheaper to build a levy on the river than it was to build 20 miles of freeway ten feet higher.

"Rivers flood, it's in their nature," Jean, the office manager, snarled. "Why is that so hard to understand?"

She was right. The higher the dam or levy is, the bigger the flood will be once it floods. And rivers always flood. Flooding is in the nature of rivers and they will always win eventually. The only issue is how much. Each year the floods gradually became worse until in 2007 the flood covered the whole freeway for several miles, shutting down the main line of travel between LA and Canada.

- Floods can be made worse by flood control.
- Debt is caused by borrowing money, directly or indirectly, to pay or offset debt.
- Arguments are usually caused by trying to settle the argument.
- Wars are caused by trying to force peace.
- Conflict is caused by trying to resolve the conflict.

So in these cases, and many more like them, the solution – the effort to solve the problem – simply makes it worse. Thus **the fewer problems we solve, the fewer problems we will have**. If we don't perceive them as problems to be solved they are simply facts of life to be addressed, which is much easier.

I've seen this often in marriage counseling. I am a huge fan of Gottman Method therapy. One of their findings is that 66% of conflicts in relationships are not resolvable. The model is designed to help people negotiate and deal with those differences, to learn how to live with them and not force a resolution where there is none.

It's not an accident that this is generally accepted as one of the most effective model of marital therapy if not just plain the most effective; if you don't try to solve it, it's not a problem, it's just a fact of life. Just deal with it.

Again, the fewer problems you try to solve the fewer problems you will have. Trying to solve problems as often as not causes more of them.

William wanted to be an attorney. He saw it as a path to wealth and power. A chance to be more marketable, a chance to be more able to demand what he wanted and to get it.

However, he wasn't a good enough student to get into one of the better law schools, so he went to a state supported one, and not one of the better state supported ones. He wasn't a good enough student to get any scholarships so he got student loans and borrowed money from his parents.

When he got out of law school he wasn't offered any jobs so he got his parents to cosign a loan for him to start his law practice. They ended up refinancing their home when the loan wasn't enough.

He met a woman who was impressed with his law practice, the nice car he drove, and his lifestyle. He neglected to tell her the money was all borrowed.

They bought a house by using her savings as the down payment. When she learned that he'd refinanced the home several times to support his practice she was incensed.

In the end it came out that he'd never turned a profit in fifteen years of practice. He'd drained all the money from his parents' equity in their home, the equity in the home he owned with his wife, and all of their credit.

"I don't understand what she is so upset about," he told me. "Everyone has to have a credit line to run their business. That's how it always has been."

As to lying to his wife about their situation he explained "If I told her she'd just blow up and not let me do it, and I would have lost my business."

It was a case of solutions which made the problem worse. He picked a profession he wasn't qualified for and ignored an increasing amount of information that he was doing something wrong.

The financial problems caused by his choice of professions led to borrowing to pay debt and to live an unrealistic life style, which led to more debt.

And then, in order to save his marriage, he lied to his wife about it hoping she wouldn't disagree with him, which didn't work.

In the end he did what he might well have done in the beginning, although it was forced on them by circumstances: they sold their house, he closed his law firm, got a reasonable job at a modest firm and began working toward being a partner. He lived within his means and the last I heard he had a reasonable relationship with his wife. Not great. She was unhappy because she'd lost the down payment she'd put into the house and this wasn't the lifestyle they'd planned on. But they were dealing with it.

They stopped solving problems and began dealing with life on life's terms. Which works better.

3. You cannot solve the problem, you can only change the paradigm which made it a problem.

I started this book out with the famous "Spoon Boy" scene from The Matrix, which, in my mind, is the whole point of the movie. You can't bend the spoon. All you can change is yourself.

This is not unlike the famous quote from Einstein that you can't solve a problem with the same thinking which created the problem in the first place. All you can change is your thinking.

There are no problems in the real world, the world of nature. Only facts of life to be addressed. Things just are the way they are. The seasons happen when they happen, the rains come and go, babies are born, sometimes babies die, people grow old, and everyone dies eventually. That's just life.

Problems only exist in the minds of people who want nature to conform to what is in their own minds. To conform to their paradigms. If what you want to happen isn't happening then you need to look inside of yourself and find out how your paradigm isn't correct, isn't accurate. You can't change nature, you cannot change the laws of cause and effect. All you can change is the way you understand them and use them.

Ask yourself;

- How are my expectations inaccurate?
- How are my ideas about cause and effect flawed or in complete?
- What is the evidence which I am ignoring?
- What are the experiences I am failing to take into account?
- What are the flaws in my thinking?
- What are the flaws in my data?
- To what am I clinging?
- What would I have to give up in order to be able to learn from my experiences?
- What is the worst possible thing that would happen if I became effective?

These are the things you will have to change about your paradigm which you will have to change in order to be free from that paradigm.

SUMMARY

1. There are no problems in the real world. Problems are merely a result of your paradigm being too small or inaccurate.
2. A problem, as we humans know it, is simply a solution which lies outside of your paradigm
   a. You can't solve a problem with the paradigm which made it a problem.
   b. You have to fix the paradigm.
3. If you allow yourself to accept and absorb disconfirming information you can expand your paradigm and the solution becomes available. Thus it isn't a problem anymore, it's just a part of life.
4. That is what growth is: assimilating disconfirming information so that you can expand your paradigm.

CHAPTER FOUR

PERSONAL DEVELOPMENT AND EVOLUTION

When I was a child, I spoke as a child,
I understood as a child, I thought as a child:
But when I became a man, I put away childish things.
For now we see through a glass, darkly; but then face to face:
Now I know in part; but then shall I know even as also I am known.

1 Corinthians 13: 12, 13

Being trapped in an inflexible paradigm or identity is like being an adult trapped in the body of a child, unable to change and adapt and grow. We are stuck because in our current paradigm or identity we don't have the tools we need to run our lives in a way appropriate to our circumstances and age. We are trying to use the wrong tools.

There is nothing wrong with being a child, nor is there anything wrong with being an infant or an old person. The only problem is if we are out of synch with the reality of our lives. If we try to lead an adult life using the ideas and strategies of a child, it won't work.

There are many models of child development but our development doesn't stop at age eighteen. Consequently there are a number of models which follow the course of our development from cradle to grave, each having their own perspective, each with something to offer. I don't think any of the major models are actually wrong. Probably they are all correct, each from their own perspective. For example some emphasize what needs we are meeting at each stage, some focus on what our skills are at each stage, some on how we think at each stage, and so forth.

What they have in common is that from the day we are born to the day we die we are faced with developing and changing to adapt to changing needs and resources, changing demands placed upon us. Ideally we move gracefully through these phases, these stages, gracefully letting go of one way of being and moving on to the next.

*

There is an Irish folk song which always reminds me of this graceful process, called *"A Wild Bunch of Thyme":*

Come all ye maidens young and fair
And you that are blooming in your prime
Always beware and keep your garden fair
Let no man steal away your thyme

For thyme it is a precious thing
And thyme brings all things to my mind
Thyme with all its flavors, along with all its joys
Thyme, brings all things to my mind

The song was explained to me as being about leading each phase of your life to the fullest. In this context thyme refers to the time of a woman's life between when she enters puberty and is no longer a little girl, but before she gets tied down to being a wife and mother.

After the young woman narrating the song has done a good job of being a child, she moves on to doing a good job of being a young woman and then finally she does a good job of being a wife and mother.

I love the deliciousness of this progress, the gracefulness of it.

My sons are now older than I was when they were born. I am now older than my father was when he died. I watched my sons grow from birth through all of their stages and now go through the stages of maturity that feel like, for me, were minutes ago. I watched my Mother watch her mother grow old and feeble and then die. Then I watched my parents pass from adulthood into old age into disability and then dementia and then death. My sons will watch me do the same. And then they will be old and their children will watch them go through the same process. Someday I will be no more than some stories about Great Grandpa Doug with the facts all mixed up.

There is no escaping the march of time and the changes we all face. We do it gracefully or un-gracefully but we can't make it go away, no matter how much cosmetic surgery we get, no matter how many red sports cars we buy or how much health food we eat.

*

Each stage of our lives is a complete paradigm.

- We have a complete list of elements and characters in our lives.
- We have a definition of who we are and who we aren't. Especially who we are vis a vis others.
- We have a list of the rules and roles by which we interact with our worlds and with the players in that world. The algorithm of what we do when, the if-then statements which govern what we do and how we interact with the world and other people.

Just because that paradigm is complete it doesn't mean that it necessarily works all that well. It might be complete but not related to our current situation. It can be chaotic or even contradictory. The rules and roles we live by can be completely wrong and lead to catastrophic results. In those cases we can't deal with life in any kind of meaningful way, we can't solve our problems or meet our needs. We can't have relationships.

We are stuck. We are using the wrong tools to deal with our lives at that particular stage.

If we can learn from our experiences and change the paradigm, adapting fluidly and gracefully, we can save our lives and move on to a more meaningful existence. If not, we are prisoners.

So we have two choices, as the old saying goes; evolve or die. Or, in this case, evolve or stay a prisoner.

*

If we look at the developmental or evolutionary stages in the various models of personal development using the model of a paradigm, it appears that they generally agree on several important points.

1) **Each developmental stage is a paradigm** as we have defined it here: a collection of the skills and resources and ideas which help us meet our needs and address the demands with which we are faced.

2) **Personal development is sequential**, meaning that we move through the developmental stages one at a time and we can't skip any.
   a) We begin with physical survival.
   b) Then survival in our families, then society, then relationships.
   c) Finally our more spiritual, individualized, transcendental needs.

3) **We only progress when we need to**. When we have to. Thus there are two requirements for us to move ahead and evolve;
   a) We achieve some degree of mastery of the skills needed at our current level. Not perfect, just as good as we are going to get at it.
   b) We are faced with needs or demands or dilemmas that simply can't be solved at our current developmental level and can only be solved by responses which exist at the next level.

I find Kohlberg's Moral Development Scale to be the best example of how this works. It's not that I think the content is better than any of the others, but the way it is assembled and the way one moves from one level to the next is, in my opinion, very useful and accurate. While the details have been refined by a half century of research, the principles have remained the same.

First of all, this isn't about the *kind* or *content* of the moral choices a person makes, but **how** they make the choice, the kind of thinking they use to arrive at their conclusions.

He posits three levels of development of two parts each. Each of them is a perfect paradigm by our definition;

1) **Preconventional,** which is divided into two parts
   a) <u>Avoiding punishment, level 1</u>. Basically this means learning how to do what is necessary to stay alive and avoid pain.
   b) <u>Getting rewards, level 2</u>. Once the individual has achieved some level of skill at staying alive they can work toward getting some of their needs met, such as food and warmth.
2) **Conventional**, which is divided into two parts.
   a) The rules and roles for being a <u>successful part of a family or small group, level 3</u>.
   b) The rules and roles for being a <u>successful member of the larger society, level 4</u>.
3) **Post-conventional morality**, in which rules are seen as practical for the well-being of society but other principles and ideals, such as human rights, may have greater importance than a slavish devotion to convention. It has two parts.
   a) <u>The social contract level, level 5</u>. At this level laws and rules are seen as social contract, not as absolutes and that the rights and needs and options of different people and groups should be respected.
   b) <u>Universal ethical principles, level 6</u>. At this level conclusions are reached based upon higher principles which supersede any one group of laws and ideas, and justice is seen as superseding the rules.

I like to illustrate this model by using the family-oriented TV series in the 1960's *The Andy Griffith Show.* The show was set in the sleepy southern town of Mayberry, about a generation earlier, and starred Andy Griffith, a small town sheriff whose wife had passed away and he was raising his son Opie, played by Ron Howard, with the help of his old maid aunt, Aunt Bea. The other two main characters were Frank the barber, who lived with his mother, and Barney (Don Knotts), the deputy sheriff and a confirmed bachelor.

Each episode was some variation on the traditional Everyman plot of nice people seeking to solve simple problems using conventional moral thinking.

Opie, as a child, had already mastered the skills of staying alive and getting rewards, and so he was a perfect Conventional Stage, level 3 person. Andy, as a sheriff, represented the morals and laws of the larger society, thus a perfect Conventional Stage, level 4 person.

Even as a child I noticed that there were no heterosexual relations in the show. None. Anywhere. There was a brief mention of a girlfriend for Andy early on, but she was never seen or named. Barney had a girlfriend who appeared once or twice but had no speaking lines.

Other than that, no one had a sexual partner or companion. It was never even alluded to.

So let's put these nice people in a moral dilemma which can't be solved with their current paradigms: Okay, it's Thanksgiving. Old maid Aunt Bea has put out a great spread for Andy, Opie, Barney and Frank. After the meal they are all sitting around talking about what they are thankful for when Barney clears his throat as if to make an announcement.

"Well, y'know," he says, trying to be casual. "We've all known and loved each other all of our lives and I don't think that anything could change how we feel about each other. So I'd just like to let you all know that Frank and I have loved each other for a long time, and we want to be a couple, to live together openly with the people we love and be accepted for who we are, based on a lifetime of love and respect and not on any preconceptions. I hope you can accept us."

This was in a complete contradiction to the morals and laws of the rural south in the 1930's, and puts them in a complete paradox between a lifetime of love and respect and their homosexuality. This is what the British faced (and failed) after World War II. Alan Turing and his famed Turing Device, the first programmable computer in the world, effectively saved Britain during WWII, and started what became the development of modern computers. Yet he was homosexual, which was illegal in Britain. Most people would have gotten at least a "thank you" for saving their country, but in this case the British government, instead of "thank you" threatened him with prison unless he took "chemical castration" drugs which ultimately led to his suicide.

So what can Andy and Opie do?

- Andy could legally arrest them and throw them in jail.
- The family could reject them and drive them out of town and never see them again.
- Andy could help Opie and himself to move to a higher level of thinking, level 5, in which the rights and needs of the people involved was more important than the convenience and the expedience of the laws.

This would be a painful experience for all involved. It would force all of them to move out of their comfort zone, even out of their reality, and into the next level of their thinking.

The only option they could never have is the option of seeing the world the same ever again.

*

Right now, if you are feeling stuck, it is because you are facing the equivalent of this story, the equivalent of being faced with such a dilemma. You are faced with the choice between everything you've ever known and everything you want to be. You can't have both.

It might be a move from being a dependent person to being the person people depend on, it could be a move from being in a world with right and wrong into a world of grey, or plaid. It could be something medium sized, like a change in profession, or something large like leaving your family and everything you have ever known.

It doesn't matter how large the dilemma is, because they don't come in sizes. All dilemmas are the same. You can't not choose. You can't choose to stay the same.

You will remain in this struggle, this conundrum, until you move to the next level of development, the next paradigm up the scale. The next identity.

Jurgen had been passive his whole life. Usually it worked pretty well. While he hadn't achieved everything he'd ever wanted, he'd achieved enough to be generally content. He'd been briefly married to a woman who was anything but passive. He'd eventually acquiesced to everything she demanded of him but, as is usually the case in these situations, the marriage ended.

Rather than fight her in court he passively allowed her to get full custody and full decision making. His son was everything to him in life and he was happy with whatever time he got with him.

Then he was faced with a dilemma. His former wife was making decisions which directly affected his son's health in a negative way, and could lead to long term health problems. Yet Jurgen had signed away medical decision making.

He could confront her with his concerns and end up in a legal battle, which terrified him, or let his son's health fail.

There was no middle ground. Both choices were out of character for him.

Rather than make either choice he stopped coming in. He left with great anger and emotion. I don't know which he chose, but clearly there was no way to stay the same.

*

Our focus in this book is on the process of moving out of our old paradigm and on to the next one – escaping from the prison of our paradigm or identity – so the focus here will be on the last point. Changing when we are faced with needs and demands that can't be addressed at our current developmental level, our current paradigm.

This will require four steps on our part;

1. Maximize our awareness of our current paradigm.
2. Maximize our discomfort with being there
3. Become acutely aware of what it is that you want or need to do which lies outside of your current paradigm
4. Make the change.

1. **MAXIMIZE YOUR AWARENESS OF YOUR CURRENT PARADIGM and how it imprisons you.**

All change is a change of paradigm, so this will apply to all change in all parts of your life.

What we have done so far in the book has been to increase your awareness of the paradigm or identity which imprisons you. Which limits you. You need to be willing to take the time, make the effort, to become intimately aware of your prison. The thoughts, ideas, beliefs and identifications to which you are clinging and, in that clinging, holding you back.

The more detail the better.

Oliver was a brilliant but terribly frightened young scientist. In spite of an impressive resume and many promotions he lived in fear of making a mistake or offending someone or not being smart enough. The range of activities he allowed himself to engage in, whether professional, personal, social or even hobbies, got smaller and smaller each year and his anxiety went up and up.

Traditional interventions met with increasing levels of internal resistance.

By focusing on the minutia of his resistance he was eventually able to articulate that if he was to become comfortable and happy that would violate three generations of his family's traditions and identity. "That just isn't who I am, that isn't what people from my family do!" Seeing the world in dangerous, catastrophic terms had long been the basis of his family's reality.

He likened his experience of being himself to the movie The Truman Show *which starred Jim Carey. In this movie the main character was trapped in an enormous dome which was really a giant sound stage in which he was the star. He wasn't allowed to know he was trapped, he wasn't allowed to know that his whole life was merely a role in a drama. He had to play out his role without ever knowing he was playing out a role.*

74

The closer he got to the way out, the periphery of the dome, the more catastrophic the reminders were that beyond the dome lay death and horrible things. There were drowned people in the river, traffic wrecks on the road, and so forth.

"That's what it's like for me. If I even imagine any other way of being I have a tremendous fear of losing who I am. Losing my whole family identity."

For quite a while his therapy consisted of either testing his limits to discover what the resistance was – the walls of the prison of his identity – or simply articulating his resistance.

Then, very slowly, he began testing to see if his catastrophic fears were real and very, very slowly he began learning that they weren't.

This illustrates several principles of change in this model.

- Resistance tends to exist only in its battle with us. When we stop fighting it and instead embrace it and acknowledge it and study it, it loses much of its power.
- It is a valuable source of information about the specifics of the way our identity prevents us from growing and changing.

Use any method you can to become aware of the details of the paradigm or identity confines and limits you. Earlier in the book I had some examples of exercises you can use to find out the beliefs about yourself which might limit you. Don't resist your resistance: take the time to listen to it and make note of it and become familiar with it. Don't fight it.

Go back to page 8 and do the exercise again, but this time with more ideas that you have gained from reading the book so far. With more insight. Focus on your resistance to the exercises and the negative feelings that come up. Make note of them, scrawl them on the page, or say them out loud. Whatever comes more naturally to you.

I am _____

I am _____

I am _____

I am _____

I am _____

I am _____

When Karen did this exercise in therapy she was startled.

*"I just realized that I **have to** be nice to everyone. I have **no** choice. That is who I have to be. I **have to** put myself last. I'm afraid that if I don't act that way I'll stop being **me**."*

*

When Kenneth did this exercise he was shocked to realize that almost all of his self-statements were negative.

*

Enid realized that all of her statements were just plain wrong!

"I identify with being a good mother, but I'm a terrible mother! I said I'm a good wife, but the fact is I'm not. I can't see how he could stand me. I just realized that I can't live up to my ideas about who I am so I give up! I have to live in a fantasy world to think I can be those things, and that's why I can't do anything right. I'm in a fantasy world."

2. MAXIMIZE YOUR DISCOMFORT RELATED TO BEING THERE.

This probably seems counter intuitive. Most books about psychology and self-help and change and growth focus on positive thinking and feeling better. However this is not the time or place for feeling good. This is the time and place for feeling bad. Not bad about who you are, but feeling bad about being stuck. Feeling bad about being in an imaginary prison.

You need to feel bad about these limitations, the limitations imposed by your identity or paradigm or self, until the pain of staying the same is greater than the pain of changing. This is no different than starting the budgeting process by finding out where you are spending money, or starting a health program by finding out the state of your physical health.

What is the price you are paying for not letting yourself change and grow? What have you missed in life so far and what are you going to miss by clinging to an identity or a way of relating to the world which no longer works for you?

I am _____

But I could be _____

I am _____

But I could be _____

I am _____

But I could be _____

I am _____

But I could be _____

I am _____

But I could be _____

I am _____

But I could be _____

And now pick one of the things you missed by clinging to your old paradigm. Something you really wish you had allowed yourself to experience.

- It might be a lost relationship or one which you never pursued.
- It could be a lost opportunity or untaken path.
- It could be something you let slip through your fingers.

Clarissa was very athletic and an aggressive executive in the financial world. She had always been told by her family that she wasn't feminine enough, that she would never be a good wife or mother. In the middle of marriage counseling with her new husband she burst out crying.

"I just realized that I'm forty five!" she wept. "I've been putting off having kids until I had just the right situation, but now that I have a good marriage if I had kids now I'd be retired before they graduated from college! I'd be changing diapers when I was fifty!"

*

Norton had grown up in a hard living blue collar family and had always identified with those roots, rejecting what he considered to be the bourgeois attitudes of the materialistic middle class. He believed that he was a warrior for the rights and values of the ordinary working class people. He took pride in his minimalist existence and when his various wives and children left him because they couldn't take it anymore, he blamed them for being too materialistic.

Then, in his late 40's he ran into a childhood friend who welcomed him into his modest home with open arms. He hadn't been "materialistic" in any way that most people would consider to be materialistic, but he had a nice home and family and his wife and kids were happy and well taken care of. He'd simply done what most husbands and fathers would do to provide for their families.

"I could have had that," Norton said sadly. *"But I had to be a jerk about everything. I could have had it all."*

Fill your heart and mind with it. Let yourself really feel what it would have felt like to have taken that step, and how deeply bad it feels because you didn't. Allow yourself to feel all the grief and loss attached to that lost possibility. This is the only legitimate use of regret: to learn from your experiences so you don't repeat them. Just know that this is the price you pay for staying the same, staying in the same paradigm

Don't cling to the pain and grief, but instead just let it flow through you until your heart and soul process it and digest it and goes its own way, it goes to the past. Feel the physical sensations of the grief and pain and loss and avoid rationalizing it. If possible don't even give it a name, until eventually your body digests and metabolizes the feeling and it becomes the energy you need in order to change.

When I was in high school I was offered a science scholarship to the University of Chicago bur I didn't pursue it because it was beyond my definition of who I was, an insignificant kid from Shoreline. Instead, I went to a very unremarkable community college near my home. When I think back on the opportunities I missed by clinging to that identity it makes me sad. I have to let myself feel that sadness because it keeps me honest when new opportunities come along. There have been many, many times when, because I hadn't dealt with the pain and loss of missed opportunities, I missed more. I rationalized and took the familiar path.

I need to let myself feel and grieve each of them as they occur, and each time I remember them, so that I remember how bad it feels to stay stuck in the old identity, the old paradigm. By remembering the pain of staying stuck, I have been able to embrace more growth and change, more joy, in the last five years than in the previous thirty years.

*

I need to be sure to note at this point that if one is new to this sort of thinking it is possible to misunderstand the difference between letting oneself grieve these losses with wallowing in self-pity or, worse, becoming depressed or defeated.

That can happen if you don't do the process of feeling bad correctly. Although I go into this in more detail in my books *The Art of Feeling Bad Correctly* and *Searching Your Soul: A Guide to Looking in the Right Places,* I need to make a few points here to prevent unnecessary suffering.

Give your feelings the respect and attention they deserve. When you are grieving or feeling your dark, sad, or complex feelings, don't multi-task. Take an opportunity to be alone and undistracted even if only for a few minutes. Give this activity your undivided attention and don't be in a hurry. No distractions.

You can always stop. Especially if you are new to this process or have had traumatic experiences you may feel overwhelmed and the feelings could become yet another trauma. If you become overwhelmed or flooded, if you feel panic that you can't contain, feel free to stop the exercise and start over another time or with the assistance of a trusted other, such as a religious leader or therapist or elder of some kind.

Remember that your feelings and thoughts are just that, feelings and thoughts. For example if I feel like a failure, that doesn't mean I am a failure. I need to feel that feeling completely and thoroughly but I need to know that it is a feeling, not a reality. Many practices refer to cultivating the observer, the witness, cultivating the perspective of observing your thoughts and feelings with compassion, but detachment. You are the thinker, not the thought, the observer, not the observed, the feeler, not the feeling.

<u>Feel them physically.</u> Our mental feelings probably evolved from our physical feelings and then, once we developed language, we probably lost track of the physical nature of our feelings. This is an opportunity to feel your feelings physically. Feel the physical sensations completely and thoroughly.

<u>As much as possible don't give your feelings a name.</u> It's interesting to note that many feelings with different names, such as fear (a "negative" feeling) and excitement (a "positive" feeling) are actually the same physically. They only differ in the name we give them. Consequently we can often confuse ourselves by reacting to the name we give our feelings rather than the feelings themselves. Often we lock a feeling in by giving it a name which prevents it from growing and changing and being processed. Try to avoid giving it a name and just feel it.

<u>Do not resist or judge your feelings.</u> Most of the time resisting pain increases the pain unnecessarily. Let the feelings flow through you like water, unresisted. Let the wisdom of your mind and body and soul do their work. The feelings won't kill you. Let them flow. Let them be processed.

<u>Let them change.</u> It is the nature of feelings to change. If we feel a feeling correctly it will almost immediately begin to change and transform. Anger turns into fear turns into loss turns into grief turns into acceptance turns into peace. Sometimes hatred is actually attraction, or dependence is actually hostility. You don't know until you simply let nature run its course and the feelings are allowed to transform and be digested and become a form of strength.

<u>Let them go.</u> When you are done chewing your food, you swallow it. When you are done processing or feeling a feeling, you are done, let it go. Don't cling to it any more than you would keep wearing the same clothes you wore at five years old. It doesn't fit any more. You are done.

3. BECOME ACUTELY AWARE OF WHAT IT IS THAT YOU WANT OR NEED TO DO WHICH LIES OUTSIDE OF YOUR CURRENT PARADIGM

I have heard several versions of the adage that we should all make a point of doing something out of character at least once per week in order to stay alive and supple. I agree.

This is a more specific version of this adage.

*

According to this model, we only change or develop or grow when we are faced with something that can only be responded to by being out of our old paradigm. Which can only be addressed by moving on to the next level of functioning.

What is that thing for you? What is the need or craving that can only be met by moving beyond your old paradigm? What is the situation you are faced with that can't be solved by the old ways of thinking?

Bernie had gone through every kind of addiction there was in an effort to avoid pain. Drugs, alcohol, sex, religion and therapy. The only way he could survive was to stop avoiding pain and accept that it is just a part of life. That was his next level.

*

Connie was the rescuer/enabler in a large, dysfunctional family of self-absorbed people. No matter how many times she set limits, no matter how many ways she sought to extricate herself they would just create increasingly egregious, hopeless situations which would force her to give up more of her life. "I have to choose between my happiness and their happiness. If I don't take care of them, they will reject me." Her next level came when she gave up any pretense of ever being accepted by them and pursued her own life oblivious to their machinations.

82

*

Dennis was a hopelessly modest young man who always followed the rules and knew his place. He was never aggressive or presumptuous and always accepted what was offered to him without complaint. He never expected anyone to take him into consideration, so they didn't. One by one all his friends and coworkers moved on to happier lives until he was alone, broke and friendless. "I can't live this way!" His next level was to stop being passive and go out and create the life he wanted.

Go back to the last exercise and look at the "but I could be…." part. What are all the things you would like to be? Need to be? Could be?

Some things aren't physically possible, such as being able to flap my wings and fly to the moon, but actually, even wanting something like that is a form of self-sabotage. I am sixty five at the time of this writing, so I can never make the "Best and Brightest Under Forty" list. But, again, even wanting something that requires changing the space/time continuum is self-destructive.

However, short of things that are physically impossible, we can allow ourselves to use our big brains and find ways to incorporate what we need and want into our next level.

We have to know that we need it and want it.

- *Charlie had always wanted to be a doctor, but couldn't because of finances and, frankly, grades. He wanted to think of himself as a doctor, but his image of himself was as a loser, damned to blue collar work. He realized he'd never let go of his dream, but, at forty five, that wasn't realistic. However, when he let himself want it as much as possible he realized he could become an EMT which was close. By letting himself know that he wanted it he was able to motivate himself to do it. He loved it.*
- *Emily wanted to be a lawyer, it was always her dream. But she was, in her mind, not that smart, not that kind of person. She stopped wanting it consciously. Then, when*

she let herself realize that she wanted it she began to think. She realized there was a way only by wanting it badly enough. The first step was to become a paralegal. She would take the rest a step at a time. And she did.

- *Hal had been obese all of his life. He wanted more than anything in the world to be a hard body. But he couldn't see it, he couldn't visualize it. He was so out of shape he couldn't work out and had been stuck at that point for years. So he made himself stop wanting. However, once he was able to acknowledge how much he wanted it he got systematic. His first step came when he decided to eat all the salad he could hold before every meal. His next step was to start parking further and further from his office. The rest of the steps fell into place.*

4. MAKING THE CHANGE

The science of change is actually more well-known than you might think. My favorite model for such change is *Change for Good* by Prochaska, Norcross and DiClemente.

In this model, based upon decades of research, change occurs in six stages;

1. Precontemplation; not yet considering the need to change.
2. Contemplation or actually considering the change and what that would mean.
3. Determination or commitment to the change, preparation and planning.
4. Take action and implement the change.
5. Maintaining the change.
6. The change is completed.

1. **Precontemplation**. If you are reading a book about freedom and change you are probably already considering that a change might be in order, might be possible. To some degree you are already unhappy with the way things are and you are considering what you might want more, you might want to be free of your old encumbrances. So you probably are already in the next phase; contemplation.

2. **Contemplation.** This is what we have been doing so far in the book. Talking about how you have limited yourself to your old definitions and identities and how you might want them to change. A common example is the case of someone who is addicted to substances. It is easy to say "I want to stop" but in this stage they would actually be thinking about what that would look like in practice. Being clean and sober around friends who are clean and sober, for example. Another common example is people who want to lose weight actually considering what that would entail, what excuses they could no longer make and how their lives and social lives might change.

At this point you would naturally be focusing in on the specific changes you would make if you were free, as we did in the last section. What the specifics are which you would like to live. And the details are important. You need to be able to see it and smell it and feel it.

3.   Determination or commitment to the change, preparation and planning. This is where we are now in the process: making a commitment to the change, making a detailed plan, knowing what you need to do.

The step to take at this point is to go over the list of things you would like to do if you were free to change – which you are – and put them together into a clear, coherent description of the you, the identity, in the next phase of your life. What the categorical changes would be. And then rank order them, put them in a list of what comes first, what the first step would be. It is often good to start with the easiest, least complicated, most accessible change. The quantitative changes.

> *I had a man who was so shy and socially withdrawn that he ate lunch alone in his office every day. He would have liked to have been a social animal, going out for lunch with others, having a social life, hobbies, and friends. That would have been his categorical change, his change of paradigm or identity. We had to pick steps, all of which were outside of his comfort zone, outside of his old identity.*
> *We had to put the steps in order; first, he had to eat lunch alone in the cafeteria until that became comfortable, then eating lunch at a table with others until that became comfortable, then interacting with them, then asking one person out for lunch, etc.*
>
> *
>
> *I had a woman who lived in a coarse, masculine world in which nothing feminine was tolerated. She wanted to be pretty and feminine now that she no longer lived in that world. Her long term goal for qualitative change, categorical change was to live a life where she could bask*

in her femininity without fear or shame. However that was too big a change for her to do all at once.

She picked one thing outside her old identity, with which to start; a manicure. However, even that turned out to be too big a first step. She was ashamed of her working-man's hands. So the first step was to get expensive, feminine hand cream and use it daily until she felt good enough to take the step of getting a manicure.

It is important to note that even getting feminine hand cream was a categorical change. It was her "one thing out of character" which had her going in the right direction.

Part of the planning part is to find social supports for your changes. For example, in the case of the shy man he had to pick co-workers he knew liked him and would respond well to him being more open. In the case of the woman wanting to become more feminine, she had to pick friends and acquaintances who would be supportive of the change, not her old friends who would ridicule her.

It is crucial in this phase to visualize and imagine these changes until they become natural to you. Until they become part of the new you, your new identity.

4. Take action and implement the change.

Eddie described himself as being poor white trash growing up in Tennessee. He worked his way through high school, college and graduate school as a carpenter and manual laborer. He had to be extremely austere, even rigid, to pursue his goals. He had to deny himself the pleasures and past times of other people his age. He always admired and resented the black community, with their rich traditions of music and spirituality. He wanted to play guitar and be a blues player. But he felt the he couldn't "take my eye off the prize". So he suppressed those feelings.

By the time he attained his professional goals he was in his forties, alone, sad and regretful. He wanted to be an exuberant, outgoing person but didn't know where to start.

He had never considered doing the things he wanted to do, being the person he wanted to be. Once we got through that phase he began to seriously contemplate the person he wanted to be, the things he wanted to be and do. Just for the sake of convenience, we started with the guitar.

The first step was for him to buy the recordings of the music he wanted unit he boiled it down to specifically the kind of music he wanted to play. Then the guitar. Then the guitar teacher he wanted.

Then one day the planning was over and it was time to start. Characteristically of him, he quickly went from buying the recordings to going to small venues and concerts of people who shared his passions and feelings. He jumped ahead to buying the guitar he wanted, one he saw in a small blues club. "I thought I'd get a cheap guitar and move up, but that would have been the old me. I got the Martin."

The hard part was when he started his lessons. It was harder than he thought. We worked hard to keep him on task, to survive the disappointments.

He made a huge step forward by learning four or five songs and playing them at open mike in a tiny venue where none of the people were better than him. Everyone there were friends and fellow travelers.

He had made the categorical change to the new paradigm, the new identity. A soulful, right brained person.

His final words to me were "Blues isn't a place you get; it's the way you get there."

In this phase, once you have made a plan for the things you want to do in your new identity, your new paradigm, you make a commitment to doing it and you do it. Not helter-skelter, but systematically, deliberately, purposefully, consciously. Watching how you are doing it and letting the changes sink in, letting the changes become part of you. Watching your old prison slip away and fade into the distance.

I need to state again that is important to have a support group of people who are congruent with the changes. As in the example, above, he didn't just learn guitar, but became part of the blues community of people who supported his new style. His fellow scientists generally weren't into the delta blues, but some of them were supportive of his new creativity and joy in life. So, systematically build a world in which you can be the you that you want to be, that you have always been but haven't been able to be.

And do it. Consciously, deliberately, with awareness.

5. **Maintenance.** Nothing stands still in life. Everything is constantly changing. Whatever the changes you make with your new freedom will only last to the extent that you consciously live an awakened, free life. You have to be aware of the temptation to slide back to the old limitations, the old prison of your old identity, but maintain your mindfulness, your awareness. Continue to cultivate your new sense of self and in that cultivation let it grow.

> Tresa had been an overweight teenager and avoided boys because it made her feel bad about her appearance. She generalized her low self-esteem to all the parts of her functioning. She married a nice man who saw her for who she was in spite of her appearance.
>
> Then a car wreck left her disabled and in great pain. What finally "pushed my button" was when she learned that she couldn't take care of her children because of her broken body. She dove into her physical therapy with a dedication that she'd never shown ever before in her life, in any part of her life.
>
> "I always survived by giving up," she explained. "Now I wouldn't give up. It was like a DNA change."

Not only did she pursue her own physical therapy to the point where she exceeded all reasonable limits, but went on to become a body-builder and had a very successful career as a physical therapist and motivational speaker for injured people.

I met her because her new role as super Mom and super wife didn't fit in a marriage in which she was the designated disabled person.

"We need to change the marriage so it is okay for both of us to be successful," she explained. They were having conflicts because the old definition of their roles didn't work. She would worry that she would revert to the old way of being – self-loathing – and that it would sabotage all she'd gained. And they fixed it!

In this example she had a long maintenance phase while the new identity and all its implications sunk in.

6. **Completion.** I don't know if I can articulate a criteria for when you can say the changes are done because I'm not sure we are ever "done". When we move from being an infant to being a toddler, being a toddler is not the finished product. Nor when we move to being a latency-stage child, nor adolescent, nor young adult, nor any of the stage. Ideally we are always in the maintenance stage until the next change becomes necessary.

In some changes, such as addictions or phobias, or specific behaviors, yes, there is a time when you are officially sober and don't have to take steps to stay sober any more. Or you are officially no longer afraid of public speaking, or officially not overweight. However, in some cases even that is controversial.

I'd be much more inclined to say that there is a time when you can say you've met the goals for this particular project and move on to the next one.

Signs and symbols

When we graduate from any level of education we are given a diploma and usually something which says "the rights and privileges accordant hereunto." When we get married we get a ring. When we pass the driver's test we get a license. Whether it's a Bar Mitzvah/Bat Mitzvah or a fraternity initiation, there is a visible process which designates the change.

In most traditions there are signs and symbols which designate transitions from one level to the next.

As our culture has become more secular, and let go of so much of our past, we have given up many of the signs and symbols which designate "you have moved on."

So we need to do it for ourselves.

- In his book "Ordeal Therapy" Jay Haley gave an example of a man, a former rock star, who was giving up his old rock star ways and committing to his family. His sign/symbols included cutting off his long hair and burying it in a coffin in a special. His short hair was a consistent reminded that he wasn't going to "party like a rock star" any more.
- One man made his 1-year sobriety coin into the fob on his key ring.
- There is a tiny chapel on Highway Two, just big enough for one person. I had a client who drove past it once a week for work. He made a commitment, which he followed, to stop each and every time to go inside and just meditate for a minute or two.

What would be the sign or symbol for you that you that you have left the old identity, the old paradigm, behind? What would remind you that you are no longer in Truman's dome?

SUMMARY

1. Personal development is a process of moving from one developmental stage or paradigm to the next.
2. The process for doing so requires that we achieve relative mastery of the skills at our developmental level and then be faced with needs and demands which can't be met at that level.
3. To expedite this process we need to maximize our discomfort with being confined to our current level of functioning and maximize our desire for what lies beyond.
4. We can also expedite the process by using the six stages of change model to make our changes specific and effective.

CHAPTER FIVE

THE LIFE OF AN UNSTUCK PERSON, A FREE PERSON

*"Eternal vigilance is the
price…of liberty"*
-   *Andrew Jackson*

Health of all kinds is not a destination, it's a way of life. Physical, mental, emotional, spiritual, financial, and relationship health are not like buying a hammer or watching a movie where you do it and it's done. It's something which is incorporated into everything you do. An ongoing process, consisting of everything you think and say and do. Not just when things fall apart, but on an ongoing basis.

- I have some friends who are in the medical professions. They keep track of every number relevant to their health. Every condition and symptom. Every nuance. They watch everything they eat and drink and breathe. They hang out with other people who care about the same things and do the same things. As a result they are very healthy. It's their way of life.

- I have other friends who are quite affluent. They read books and newspaper articles about money. They watch money related TV shows. They keep track of their money to the penny on a daily basis. They hang out with people who work with money. They talk about money. It's their way of life.

- I have another group of friends who are very spiritual. They go to spiritual events, talk with other people who are spiritual and do spiritual things. Their lives are serene. Their jobs are serene. It's their way of life.

*

I think it would be safe to say that there has been enough research done that we know how to make more money, have better sex, raise great children, or have perfect health if we just read the books and just plain did it. No resistance. Just read the books, follow the programs and just do it. Some programs are better than other, but most of them will work if you do them. Period.

The simple reality is that most of us, most of the time, don't. We can have it if we do it. I'm sure there are details which make one plan better than another, faster, easier, or better results, but in pretty general terms we can have it if we do it, we can't if we don't.

The same applies to freedom, peace, and Un-Stuckness. It has been researched for thousands of years. If we practice it as a way of life it will work. There are dozens, probably hundreds of models. Each one slightly different, each with its own focus or spin. Some are better than others. Each has its own results or outcomes. The following are just some of the ideas I know about. I will have more next week, and more still in ten years. If you do your own reading and soul searching, you will come up with more, too. These are some of the long term traits and practices of people and lifestyles conducive to staying Un-Stuck, adapting and changing in a fluid, conscious manner.

The following suggestions for how to stay Un-Stuck are;

1. Everything begins with wanting.
2. Living consciously and deliberately: being aware.
3. Compassion, connection and community.
4. Don't let your life lead you.
5. Discipline, and deliberateness

1.   Everything begins with wanting: The Art of Wanting Correctly.

The second of the Four Noble Truths of the Buddha can be understood as saying that unnecessary suffering is caused by wanting incorrectly and the third of the Four Noble Truths is that by learning how to want correctly, without clinging or craving, we can minimize unnecessary suffering.

The Christian Bible, especially the Sermon on the Mount, is full of good advice about the correct way of wanting and appears to largely agree with the Buddha.

I'm sure every religion and psychology has some reference to the idea that wanting is an art and the better you are at it the better your life will be. In current clinical psychology, under a variety of names, quite a bit has been researched and written on the subject.

At the very foundation of psychology is the phenomena that our behavior is motivated. That it is, in other words, the result of wanting. Everything that we do or think is motivated by its ability to meet our various needs. And what does motivation mean except wanting? If you don't want something you aren't motivated to get it. If you do want it, you will change your behavior to get it.

*

In other words, everything in your world is the result, directly or indirectly, of what you wanted[4]. This isn't to say that you wanted it, only that it is the *result* of what you wanted. For example no one wants to grow up to be a drug addict. However, if you want to avoid the pain and suffering of life, that will lead you to avoidant behavior, such as the various addictions, because we do those things to avoid pain. The inevitable addiction and suffering, then, is the result of what you wanted; to avoid pain. The same would apply to living beyond our means. No one wants to be broke, but we might want to have things we can't afford, so being broke can be the result of our errors of wanting.

---

[4] The exception is things that were done to you as a child over which you had no control or influence.

So we are back to my point: everything in your life is the result, directly or indirectly, of what you wanted. The things that are in your life that you don't want are the result of wanting incorrectly. So if wanting has such an enormous effect on our lives if behooves us to learn how to do it well in order to minimize our suffering.

*

There appear to be three kinds of wanting incorrectly;

1.   Wanting which is inconsistent with the universe.
2.   Craving.
3.   Ambivalence.

*

Wanting which is inconsistent with the universe.

The natural laws of the universe are inviolable:
Energy condenses into substance. Food is eaten through
the mouth and not the nose.
A person who neglects to breathe will turn blue and die.
Some things simply can't be dismissed.
It is also a part of the cosmic law that what you say and
do determines what happens in your life. The ordinary
person thinks that this law is external to himself and he
feels confined and controlled by it. So his desires trouble
his mind, his mind troubles his spirit, and he lives in
constant turmoil with himself and the world. His whole
life is spent in struggling.
The superior person recognizes that he and the subtle
law are one. Therefore he cultivates himself to accord
with it, bringing moderation to his actions and clarity to
his mind. Doing this, he finds himself at one with all that
is divine and enlightened. His days are passed drinking in
serenity and breathing out contentment.
This is the profound, simple truth: You are the master of
your life and death. What you do is what you are.

Hua Hu Ching # 40

In his documentary *Quantum Activist,* Dr. Amit Goswami, Ph.D, in the context of discussing manifestation, a subject akin to wanting, answered the perennial question "I tried to manifest/want a new BMW and it didn't happen. What did I do wrong?"

He used several examples of people wanting things which contradicted the laws of nature or the will of the universe. Such as both baseball teams wanting to win, when, in fact, that isn't possible. Or wanting eternal youth, or to win the lottery every time you buy a ticket.

It's not that there is anything necessarily wrong with wanting those things, so much as it could extrapolate out into a physical impossibility, like my earlier example of flapping my wings and flying to the moon, or winning "The Best and Brightest Under Forty" when I'm 65. That's not how the universe works.

The universe is an orderly place and governed by the laws of reality. If we expect the universe to change its laws, just for us personally, we will be disappointed. We won't win, no matter how hard we try to beat it. If, as the above quote suggests, we learn to want in a way which is harmonious with the universe, we have a better chance of getting what we want and a wonderful chance of being peaceful and harmonious and able to grow and change smoothly.

- If I want to diet and exercise until I lose weight, then that is working with the laws of the universe. If, instead I want to eat anything I want and wake up in the morning looking like a magazine cover, then that flies in the face of medical reality.
- If I want to get a raise just because I am so cool, that flies in the face of the laws of the universe. If I want to be able to do the things it takes to get a raise, then that is working with the laws of the universe.

So if you want to live the life of a supple person who adapts smoothly and fluidly, learn the art of wanting correctly, working in collaboration with the universe and not surrendering your life to struggling. Make it a part of your lifestyle to always ask yourself if your intentions are congruent with the laws of the universe or contradict it? Take time to consider how you could learn how to want in a manner more congruent with the laws of the universe, more consistent with reality.

Craving: You can never get enough of what you don't want.

Many translations of the Four Noble Truths use the term "craving" to describe wanting incorrectly. What is the difference between craving and wanting? Other than casual interposition of the words they are actually very different.

My whole life I have loved working in the yard. Back when we moved into a new house when I was in my 30's I would get up first thing in the morning, have a quick breakfast, and go work in the yard for hours, living on diet cola. If at all possible I wouldn't even take food breaks.

One day we didn't have any diet cola so I got a can of diet root beer, which is about the same thing. Right? However, within an hour or so I was craving another, so I got another and drank it quickly. However my thirst wasn't satisfied! I found myself getting a third can which I couldn't drink because I was so full, yet still craving more. This didn't make any sense.

Then I realized that what I was craving was the caffeine, which cola has and root beer doesn't. I had a cup of coffee and I was fine.

You cannot get enough root beer to meet your craving for caffeine!

A common example of craving is when someone confuses sex with love and in an effort to find love has more and more sex, with less and less satisfaction of their need for love. Or when people want to be rich, so they borrow the money to appear rich, which only increases the anxiety which they think being rich would alleviate.

- No amount of sex can meet your need for love.
- No amount of debt can meet your need for financial security.
- No amount of external beauty can meet your need for internal beauty.
- No amount of screaming, adoring fans can meet your need for parental approval.

The simple test for craving is, if you get it, are you satisfied?

If the answer is yes, it isn't a craving. You are just meeting a need.

If the answer is no, you want more, then it is a craving. You are wanting more and more of what isn't really what you want or need. Be willing to ask yourself this question about everything you want.

If you go down this road the cravings will take your life over and lock you into a lifestyle which will preclude any kind of healthy adaptation or growth.

To be a fluid, free, adaptive person you need to be attuned to what you are wanting, constantly asking yourself, is this what I really want? Is this really meeting a healthy need in me? If it isn't, then you need to be willing and ready to change your strategy such that you only want things that meet your needs, and you want the things that, in fact, do meet those needs. So that you don't waste your time and energy on things that don't meet your needs.

My wife and I went boating with a friend yesterday. He loves his boat and spends hours working on it, playing on it, and getting ready to work or play on it. It's in factory-new condition at all times.

As we pulled out of the marina we noticed that about a quarter of the boats have not been moved or cleaned in ten years. Some are literally covered with the filth of age. Given the cost of a slip in a private marina, and the cost of the boats, those people are spending a lot of money on something that meets no needs! A hobby in name only!

Ambivalence

Go away closer and stop it some more!
I do/don't want/don't want to be/not be with you/somebody else
For the rest of my life but not a minute longer!
So shut up and tell me what you think!

Ambivalence is when you have two contradictory feelings about something. Ambi=two or more, valence=value.

*

There are two really good books on this subject, *Changing for Good*, which I've already cited, and *Motivational Interviewing*[5]. What they both point out is that one of the biggest obstacles to change is our ambivalence, our unarticulated resistance to what we think we want. It is a form of wanting incorrectly. Until we resolve this ambivalence we will be trapped, stuck, and unable to proceed or move in a productive way.

As I mentioned above the problem is not a shortage of good solutions to our problems, the problem is our lack of actually *doing* them. Most of the time this is rooted in ambivalence, wanting incorrectly. Wanting in a contradictory manner.

Commonly cited examples are;

- The person who wants to lose weight but doesn't want to exercise or change their diet.
- The person who wants good grades but doesn't want to study.
- The person who wants to become more successful but doesn't want to do the things it takes to get there.
- The person who wants more friends but they don't want to have to be nice to people.
- The person who wants to be respected but doesn't want to be respectable.

---

[5] Miller and Rollnick *Motivational Interviewing, Preparing People for Change.*

The same thing applies to our personal evolution. It is easy to want in the abstract, but when the rubber meets the road we might be faced with our ambivalence, our conflicting desires or motives about what it takes to grow and change.

*

Ambivalence is the very essence of being stuck. Dealing with it is the very essence of getting Un-Stuck. Ambivalence means to be paralyzed by having opposing feelings about something. There are four kinds of ambivalence;

1. Approach/approach. This means there are two things that you want which are incompatible. For example wanting to watch a movie and go to a party, or wanting two different pieces of clothing when you can only afford one or the other.
2. Avoidance/avoidance. When there are two things you don't want but you have to choose. For example you don't want to pay your taxes but you don't want your paycheck impounded either, or you don't want to go to work but you don't want to be fired.
3. Approach/avoidance. When there is something that you want but you don't want at the same time. Many people feel this way about marriage. They want it because there are benefits but there are drawbacks to being monogamous. Or sobriety. It's easy to not want DUIs but you might not want to give up the wild parties.
4. Double approach/avoidance. There are only two possible choices, both of which you are ambivalent about. For example, wanting to be married but not wanting to be tied down, versus wanting to be single but not wanting the lack of stability.

The frequently noted phenomena of wanting half of something is an example of wanting incorrectly and it is a form of ambivalence;

- I want the job but not the work it entails.
- I want to look good but I don't want the reactions it can get.
- I want to buy the car or house but not the upkeep that they require.
- I want the money but not the work it takes to manage it well.
- I want the authority but not the responsibility which comes with it.
- I want the pizza but not the weight gain.

*

The test for ambivalence is easy; anything that you want which you've done or gotten or achieved it's because you weren't ambivalent or at least overcame the ambivalence: you just did it. Regardless of how hard it was or how long it took, you did it. If there is something that you want which you haven't gotten or done or achieved, it is because of some form of ambivalence. If you weren't ambivalent you would have just done it.

As an exercise in self-knowledge, just make a list of all of the things you say you want or think you want but haven't done.

_____

_____

_____

These are the things about which you are ambivalent. Take the time to feel and admit and articulate your ambivalence. What is it about? I have wanted to be a writer since I was ten, and I've written or at least had a good start on perhaps a dozen books. But until now I had only finished and published one.

I had to inspect my own ambivalence and I realized that it was fear of being judged. Only when I admitted and resolved that ambivalence could I move ahead and start finishing and publishing some of those books, the first of which is this one!

Learning how to see and address your ambivalence, to learn how to want correctly, is the first step of change and evolution, the first step toward being Un-Stuck, because anything you become un-ambivalent about you can do, and that, by definition, is freedom. That, by definition, is being Un-Stuck.

*

Our deepest fear is not that we are inadequate.
Our deepest fear is that we are powerful beyond imagination.

Mary Ann Williamson, *Return to Love*

This is not something to be attempted by the faint of heart! Changing your ambivalence and learning how to want correctly is a huge step, one that comes both with potential and with responsibility! Taking charge of your life and your thoughts and your actions, taking charge of your perceptions of yourself and the world and living deliberately, without ambivalence changes a lot of things! Everything! You will see yourself and the world differently, you will feel a lot of things you may have been wanting to avoid for a long, long time. You will be faced with a lot of realities you may not want to face. For example the real reasons you didn't do this sooner.

Mostly it will make it difficult if not impossible to engage in blame, denial, or projection. Which is one reason why many people are ambivalent and avoid success. They have to give up their weakness. They have to face the reality that there never really was a reason.

One of the support staff at the mental health center in the early 1980's was clearly a very good worker, very intelligent and good at everything she did. She was good with people and well respected. She was well educated, and well trained. Except she presented herself as a tramp; she wore rumpled, tattered, often unwashed men's clothes, seldom washed her hair, never set it, and chain smoked while chewing gum. Sometimes her clothes were too revealing for a mental health center setting. She didn't come across as the skilled professional she really was.

She kept applying for jobs in the private sector but never got them. She said it was because women were discriminated against. At the insistence of several of her friends she begrudgingly agreed to get a makeover and a nice suit of clothes for her next interview.

Before the interview she was in the coffee room with her friends. She looked great but was clearly upset.

"What if I don't get the job?" she asked querulously. "I might not get the job."

"It never bothered you before," her friends said. "Why does it bother you now?"

"Because I never tried that hard before. What if I get it and I screw it up?"

Giving up her ambivalence meant facing the change of actually getting a job she cared about and thus face the real – as opposed to abstract – chance of failure.

I've had many people over the years who have wanted the benefits of evolving and growing and changing but they didn't want to give up blaming other people, or they have rejected anything which would challenge their pre-existing beliefs, their religious or political beliefs.

Hector was an entrepreneur who had lost heavily in the crash and had become very depressed. He was able to see the ways in which his old definition of who he was and how the world worked had made him rigid, inflexible, and unable to adapt to modern economic times. He became more able to adapt and change. In time he salvaged his business and his marriage.

However he hit a stumbling block when it came to compassion. He completely rejected anything that had to do with compassion for others who were less fortunate, including his wife. If she felt bad about something "that's her own damn problem. Feelings are a choice. She can damn well change how she feels, after all, I changed how I feel!"

He finally left therapy on the grounds that "I'm here to help me, not anybody else. Poverty is a choice. If someone wants compassion they can goddamn well pay a therapist to have compassion for them!"

*

Homer had grown up under horrible, impoverished conditions. He made good progress in therapy for a while but when we got to the part about what he'd like to do with his life, he got dug in.

"It sounds like you are saying I'm responsible for my life. That means you are letting those other people off the hook, and I'm not buying it. I didn't cause this problem and it's not my job to fix it!"

While these two men represent opposite ends of the political/economic continuum the phenomena was the same. They were willing to change and grow only insofar as it didn't challenge their underlying beliefs. As long as it didn't challenge the way they rationalized their behavior. The issue here isn't right or wrong: it's about resistance to change.

Janice was a fundamentalist Christian referred by her pastoral counselor for treatment for her depression and her reaction to some very traumatic situations.

She didn't complete the first session.

"If what you want us to do works," she explained angrily, "that means that what my minister has been saying all these years is wrong. I believe that Christ is the only way anything can be fixed and that is that!" And she left.

As with many people she would only accept therapeutic outcomes which endorsed their prior belief systems.

You can't simultaneously want to change and want to stay the same without becoming stuck. You really have to pick one or the others. This can be a very painful process but one which can't be ignored. You may have to spend a lot of time grieving a belief system, a paradigm, a way of life, or an identity which worked fine at one time but not anymore.

It's about wanting correctly. It's about being non-ambivalent.

My preferred way to deal with ambivalence is a combination of the ideas in the above-mentioned books and the approach I'm following in this book;

1) **Don't try to change it for now**! Force only makes it worse. Categorical change only occurs through letting, not forcing.
2) Go through these steps consciously, deliberately. Preferably you set aside the time, and find a place where you can be uninterrupted to go through these steps for however long it takes, as often as you need to go through them.
3) Acknowledge the ambivalence and take responsibility for it.
   a) This means don't blame it on circumstances or other people.
      i) It was a strategy you chose at one time.
      ii) Probably for a good reason, but nevertheless you chose it.
      iii) Maybe not consciously, but you chose it.
   b) Accept that it is there because it serves a valid psychological purpose for you. Or at least it did at one time.
   c) It is protecting you from something.
4) Identify and embrace the psychological need you have for the ambivalence.
   a) Usually this is some variation of clinging to the old identity, the old paradigm or reality.
   b) Clinging to the old ways or avoiding something frightening.
5) Completely surrender to the ambivalence.
   a) Let it take you over. You might as well: it's already taken you over anyhow. It helps to do it voluntarily.
      i) Feel it as much and as thoroughly as possible.
      ii) Feel the ambivalence as physically as possible.
   b) Don't fight it.
      i) Accept that it will never go away.
6) As is almost always the case, when you completely embrace a feeling thoroughly, physically, without hesitation, it begins to change, to transform, like food when it is eaten correctly.
   a) Some people report that it is like the ambivalence has a story to tell, that it wants you to know. In these cases there could be actions you need to take to address those issues as part of resolving the ambivalence and moving on.

i) Sometimes it is about a traumatic event when you were younger that it is trying to protect you from. You may need to get involved in some sort of healing or therapy for those memories.

ii) Sometimes it is about doubts or fears or self-loathing that it wants you to be aware of. Each of these could involve a course of action.

iii) Sometimes it just wants you to be aware of an issue or something unresolved.

b) Keep this up until the opposite sides of the ambivalence become one and you are no longer ambivalent.

i) Eating and sleeping are not opposites, they are just part of a 24 hour cycle.

ii) A job and its responsibilities are different parts of the same thing. You can't have one without the other.

iii) Being nice to people is just a part of having friends, not the opposite.

iv) What you want and what you have to do to get it are one and the same.

v) Choosing to spend money on one thing is the same thing as choosing to not spend it on something else. They aren't opposites, they are part of the same thing.

vi) What you don't want and the price you have to pay to avoid it are one and the same.

7) This is the point at which you may become free from the ambivalence and can move on with your life.

a) By wanting both parts of the same thing you are wanting correctly.

Edward had worked in the family business for years. His whole life. It had always been his dream. When his Dad passed away he took it over, promising to make it what it could be.

One by one his siblings moved on to have their own careers, and he felt deserted by them. He felt like they were abandoning the family. One by one they tried to tell him that it was long overdue for closure, and that it couldn't possibly work. It no longer had a place in the market. He accused them of not believing in the family legacy.

He borrowed everything he could borrow to keep it running. He even got a second mortgage on his house to make payroll. It still kept getting worse. His wife left him and threatened to file for divorce. He still couldn't let go.

When he came in he was clinically depressed and vaguely suicidal. He couldn't bring himself to shut the business down. But he couldn't deny that it was a done deal. Everyone in his world was threatening him, demanding that he shut it down. But the harder they pushed the harder it became for him to even consider shutting it down.

Force begets resistance.

Since force didn't work I just focused on his feelings, how bad it must feel, what it reminded him of, where the feelings were coming from. Soon he began to tell me stories about the family business, growing up with their own company, feeling important. He told me what it felt like when he was a kid walking into the office and being treated like the boss's son. Then he began to tell me about his own dreams of being a factory owner, a captain of industry. Someone his Dad could have been proud of, someone his children would be as proud of as he'd been of his father.

Then it became grief. He cried and cried and cried. He cried for his dead father, he cried for his lost dreams, he cried for how bad it would feel to close the doors for the last time. He cried about

110

what it would mean to work for someone else, to not be the owner anymore. He even cried about his father's old desk!

He began to see the factory as the burden it really was, the albatross, the anchor it had been in his life.

The subject moved slowly from ambivalence to grief, from if to when, and finally how. For several sessions he talked about the legalities and financial steps one has to go through to close a business. He had already told the employees when their last paycheck would be. With more tears he rehearsed all the steps he'd have to go through until there were no more tears. It was settled and wouldn't be visited again.

Finally we came to the last issue; what he'd do from then on.

"Ten years ago I'd learned all I'd needed to learn about being a manager. I just didn't want to work for someone else. But that doesn't seem to matter anymore. It'll be a relief to not worry about payroll and line of credit and all that stuff."

He closed the business and got a nine to five job with one of his former competitors. Last I heard he was reconciling with his wife.

In order to live in an Un-Stuck manner, in order to lead a lifestyle conducive to leading a life that adapts fluidly and effectively, we need to be aware of the art of wanting correctly, wanting without ambivalence or self-sabotage. In order to do this we need to take the time to understand our own patterns of ambivalence, the things that we become ambivalent about and how to detect our ambivalence as soon as it raises its head.

We need to become articulate and conscious about what and how we want and realize that whatever we think we want, if we don't have it, the problem lies in our ambivalence.

2.   Living in a conscious, deliberate, aware manner

Being stuck is the opposite of being conscious, so it makes sense that if you want to stay Un-Stuck you would need to practice being conscious and deliberate.

*

There is a recurring metaphor that if you put a frog in a pot of boiling water it will immediately jump out. But if you put a frog in cold water and gradually turn the heat up it will very gradually be cooked alive without jumping out. When we are stuck we are like the frog who has become so accustomed to the water in the pot that it identifies with it, feels like it is normal, and is cooked alive.

This is what happens when we are not awake, when we are not conscious, deliberate or aware of what is happening in our lives and around us. We live in a world filled with drugs, alcohol, money, sex, politics, news, entertainment and beauty which can, if we let it, lull us into complacency and numbness, distract us from what is really happening in our hearts and minds and souls. That is how we got lost in the first place.

We need to make awake-ness, aware-ness as much a part of our lives as using our turn signal when we turn our car or turning off the stove when we are done making dinner.

*

What does it mean to be aware? Awake?

I like to compare it to the difference between seeing the world through a key hole compared to being out there in the wide world, seeing all of it at once. I've seen this when being in the woods with someone who is very experienced and comfortable being there compared to someone who has never been in the woods before.

The newcomer is so overwhelmed with the new stimulation that they can't see anything. Their fear and confusion clouds their perceptions. The older, more experienced person sees everything in

112

proportion. Those aren't just trees over there, they are a perfect place to string a rope and make a tent. Those aren't just a pile of twigs, they are kindling. They know from which way the rain will come and how to make a fire.

The fear of the newcomer is the same as the fear we feel when we aren't aware of what is going on around us, and the confidence of the experienced person is the opposite. It is the result of being awake and aware and seeing things the way they really are. Not being able to see things creates the fear, being able to see things creates the confidence.

Think back to a recent time when you suddenly became aware that you'd taken a wrong turn and were driving someplace you hadn't intended, or had a period of time when you weren't paying attention to what someone else was saying or doing. We've all had that happen. That was when you weren't aware. The thing that followed was awareness. Suddenly you paid attention and saw things differently. You became awake. It helps to have these comparisons so that you can notice the difference more clearly, and make informed choices about which way to be.

In the middle of conducing a therapy session the summer I was 44 I became slowly aware of the physical sensations of a heart attack; angina pain, pain down the underside of my left arm, shortness of breath, diaphoretic sweating, and weakness. Those feelings started slowly, then there was a time that I was consciously aware of them. Then a moment occurred when that was all that I could think of! Luckily it wasn't a heart attack and I got off with just an angioplasty. But there was a Moment when unawareness became awareness and everything changed. I still remember that transition.

There have been several times in my career that I realized that the way I was doing things in my business couldn't possibly work and I'd need to change my plans and expectations. That was a Moment of aware-ness; that was awake-ness. What happened before was asleep-ness.

*

There are many practices which encourage awake-ness, Un-Stuckness. I've known a number of people who I felt practiced awake-ness and they usually had many different habits and practices in their lives to make sure they were being awake. Meditation, journaling, various religious practices, self-inspection, reading, and many, many more. One such method is therapy, but it's only one. Since therapy is the one I'm most familiar with many of the references here will be to therapy, but I acknowledge that it is only one way.

One of the most important things you can use therapy for is to become awake, for me as the therapist to help my client sift through the un-aware sleep of daily life so that they can look at their lives with awake eyes, with an aware mind and see the truth of what is going on in their lives. The same applies to meditation teachers and spiritual leaders. To help us find our awake eyes. Sometimes even an aware, awake friend to talk to who can help us see ourselves and our lives accurately. To discover being deliberate. To discover that you were always making choices but didn't necessarily know it.

All of the things I wrote in the beginning of this book were methods intended to help you wake up and become aware of what you liked and didn't like in your life, how you really felt about your life and what you were doing. The inventories and questions. How did it feel to see things differently? What did you see differently? How did you do it?

*

To put it quite simply, **you saw because you looked**. You wake up only when you intentionally wake up. Dreams usually feel too good for us to automatically wake up. We have to **want** to wake up.

People with peaceful, fluid, free lives, people who evolve, are people who deliberately take the time to think about their lives, about the world, and how they relate to the world. It might be through meditation, journaling, therapy, or some other practice, but they take the time to sit and think. To be awake enough to know when something changes or isn't working. To notice when the water is boiling.

If you want to be as Un-Stuck as possible, as free as possible, find one of these practices and make it a part of your life. Not something that you do on an as-needed basis. But something like eating or sleeping, something you do as a routine part of your day, of your life.

Taking the time to sit and think and observe. A time to see. Deliberately and consciously. As part of your daily living.

- One man has Dan Segal's mindfulness exercise on his computer start-up screen so the first thing he does every day is a mindfulness exercise.
- A woman journals every night before she goes to sleep, to inventory everything she's done and thought that day.
- A businessman turns off all of his media and spends sixty seconds of silence before finalizing any serious decision.
- I know a therapist who spends one week every year in silent meditation at a local monastery.

In this way you aren't going to be the frog who cooks slowly. You will be able to say "wait a minute, this water is hot!" You won't be twenty years into a pathological relationship before you notice it, you will see it quickly and apply a fix because you are deliberately looking at your life. Consciously and deliberately.

Again, there are many methods. If you choose one or many doesn't matter. Which method you choose doesn't matter very much. Journaling, psychotherapy, confession, meditation group, drumming retreats, anything which gives you the opportunity to reflect and see your life through objective eyes. Experiment and practice and see which method works the best for you.

As long as you do it.

Do it regularly, consistently, at the same time and the same way every time. Like when the Buddha committed to sitting under the Bodhi Tree until he found enlightenment. Stick with it until you see what you are looking for.

*

Currently there is a huge awakening of interest in meditation and specifically mindfulness, a subset of meditation. I personally find both meditation, as a larger group of practices, and mindfulness specifically to be invaluable in helping us to awaken and remain conscious. It doesn't have to be esoteric or complicated.

There are several authors/speakers/teachers/researchers who have done tremendous things bringing these skills into public availability. These are four that I like, but there are more. I would suggest pursuing any or all of them to find practices which help you remain awake. Most have websites with guided meditations you can practice on your own, as well as written material;

Dan Siegel http://www.drdansiegel.com/

Ron Siegel http://www.mindfulness-solution.com

Tara Brach http://tarabrach.com/howtomeditate.html

Jon Kabat-Zinn http://www.mindfulnesscds.com

3.   Compassion, connection, community.

A good measure of being awake and aware and Un-Stuck is our ability to notice reality.

The reality is that we are all different atoms on the same molecule, different molecules in the same cell, different cells in the same finger, different fingers on the same hand, different hands on the same body, different bodies in the same species, different species in the population of the same planet, different planets in the same solar system, different solar systems in the same galaxy, and different galaxies in the same universe.

We are not separate. That is reality. We are all part of the same thing. Anything else is an illusion. The myth of separateness is an illusion. Everything that everyone does on the planet will ultimately affect everyone else in some way.

The myth that we are separate allows us to do and think and feel insane things. Insane things like selfishness, loneliness, or isolation. Insane things like violence or cruelty or exploiting others for personal gain. Insane by definition; it is not based on reality because the reality is that we are all connected. We are all equivalent.

Your pain feels the same as my pain, your fate feels the same as my fate. Your successes feel as good to you as mine do to me, and your failures taste as bitter to you as mine do to me. We all struggle with mostly the same struggles, the same pain, and the same angst.

*

This is compassion. The awareness that we are all the same, all connected, struggling the same struggles. When we can feel that and live accordingly we are aware of the pain and suffering and struggle of all people and we want to do what we can to reduce it or at least not cause more. You could no more casually cause pain to another person than you could casually cause that same pain to yourself.

117

*

We are all naked under our clothes, we were all born and we will all die at some point, and in a few million years, other than some future archaeologists, no one will much care that we ever existed. Nothing that any of us could do can increase our significance one iota. Because nothing any of us can do will be of much significance two or three million years from now. Nothing any of us could do can change our destiny or importance one iota. So why try? Why try to create specialness or separateness or entitlement when it can't possibly work? Why cause harm to one person or group of people when we are all the same?

Is there a difference between the smartest worm in the world and the dumbest? The richest ant and the poorest? The most attractive alligator and the ugliest?

Not really. The same applies to us humans if looked at from the right perspective. There really isn't anything particularly different between beautiful people and ugly people, smart people and not so smart, rich people and poor people. Not in the long run. Watch the news sometime when they are showing the aftermath of a big tornado. All those houses are leveled for miles and miles. The rich ones and the poor ones, the big ones and the little ones. All gone.

Does anyone really care who the richest cave man was? The prettiest? The strongest? So why care about any such differences in the current time? We are really all the same. We are really all equivalent.

All the reasons and excuses and methods by which we claim to be able to differentiate ourselves from each other are illusions. Illusions which allow us to feel terribly alone, which allow us to do terrible things. Illusions.

Without those illusions those terrible things would not be possible. Literally impossible.

*

That is why in almost all practices and philosophies and religions, compassion is one of the most important virtues to be pursued. Because if you are not compassionate you are on the wrong track. You are still trapped in illusions. This is one of the most important ways you can measure or assess if you are on the right track. If you are looking in the right direction.

Consequently compassion in and of itself is a virtue in that it provides better for the long term well-being of the species better than greed, **but it is also a measure of your progress**, of the direction you are going. Just like my weight, blood pressure, blood sugar and cholesterol level are measures of my physical health.

Compassion is a measure of our sanity. Our evolution. Without compassion, you are not progressing. Compassion alone is not sufficient, but its absence means you are not progressing.

*

Connection is an important aspect of compassion. It is, in some ways, the emotional experience that we are all different versions of the same thing. That we aren't separate.

I used to attend St. Mark's Episcopal Church in Seattle. An enormous old building overlooking the entire city. Its congregation reflected the mixed neighborhood it was in: elegant old money, street people, conservative business people, LGBTA people, college professors and the mentally ill. Rich and poor. Every race.

One Sunday, in the middle of a prayer, a mentally ill man wandered into the church and began ranting and raving. The priest effortlessly shifted the content of the prayer to compassion for the mentally ill man.

One of the parishioners, a long term US Representative from our area and a well-known psychiatrist, a very dignified man in a nice suit, stood up and gently put his arm around the homeless schizophrenic, and guided him to the seat next to him and comforted him, and the service went on its way.

It was the perfect connection.

Community is the manifestation of this feeling. It is in our nature to gather into communities, families, couples, unions, neighborhoods, clubs, teams, interest groups, and factions. We are constantly finding communities to attach to or identify with or to reject.

If you want to be awake, surround yourself with people who are awake or working on it. If you want to be compassionate, surround yourself with people who want to be compassionate. Whoever you surround yourself with will bring out those traits in you.

4. Don't let your life lead you.

He says, "Bill, I believe this is killing me"
As a smile ran away from his face
"Well, I'm sure that I could be a movie star
If I could get out of this place"

Now Paul is a real estate novelist
Who never had time for a wife
And he's talking with Davy, who's still in the Navy
And probably will be for life

Billy Joel, *The Piano Man*

One of the most common variable in the people I've seen and worked with over the last forty years is chaos. Not just internal, but all parts of their lives. Too many commitments, not enough time, too many unsettled issues, not enough money or energy. I think of this as the behavioral equivalent of hoarding: filling your life and time up with "stuff" so that you don't have to deal with the more important, the more subtle parts of your life. Or, even without that unconscious intent, simply having a life that is too complicated to allow change or growth or spontaneity.

Like Marley's Ghost in Charles Dickens' The Christmas Carol, we spend eternity weighted down with the cash boxes of our unfinished business. You can't change because you are too anchored to too many things that won't let you change.

George was a nice man. A very nice man, but he was buried. He and his wife had a few more kids than they intended, a few too many years apart. One was married and in college when the youngest was in grade school.

He was a good father. Actually a great father. "A Dad is who I am," he used to say. He coached several teams for his kids, helped out with Boy Scouts and Girl Scouts. He was on the board at the church, taught Sunday school, he was on the PTSA, and Neighborhood watch.

121

As his family grew up he shared with me, privately, all the dreams he'd had which he'd never be able to fulfill because he was too busy, all the things he'd wanted to do that he couldn't do, or, by the time he'd have the time to do them he'd be too old.

He shared with me that in the last twenty years his feelings about his faith had changed. He was still a believer, but his ideas had changed. However, he was too locked into his church to ever talk about or act upon those new beliefs. He was locked into his life. He was a prisoner of his life.

His feelings about his life and his family and his marriage had changed a little, but he was locked in too tightly to even think about it.

*

There was an author who wrote a very influential and timely book thirty years ago. She was giving a speech recently when some of the people tried to engage her in a controversy about the book. At one point they became enraged because she wouldn't defend the position she'd taken in the book.

"I wrote that book thirty years ago!" she exclaimed. "I've learned a lot in that time. I have no intention of being held hostage to something I know much more about now!"

She was not trapped, she did not let herself be anchored. She allowed herself to be adaptive and fluid and supple.

We can't grow or change when we are firmly anchored. Visually, when I meet someone in this situation, I see them like an elephant surrounded by people with ropes. Tiny, insignificant people. Any one of them couldn't hold an elephant, but ten or twenty could hold him down, prevent him from moving. One rope is debt, one is yard work, another is committees, another is relatives, another is a social group, another is a career, and so forth. Pretty soon you are tied down!

Sometimes the anchors are roles we have committed to.

Back in the late 1980's I was on a committee with Brock, who held a high office in local government and had since he'd graduated from college decades earlier. He'd grown with the job. He was a nice man, intelligent and well informed, but seemed to always be slightly uncomfortable.

One day I heard he was retiring soon to pursue a completely unrelated career. I had coffee with him just before he left.

"This made sense thirty years ago," he told me sadly. "And it became my career, and then it became the careers of lots and lots of people. But somewhere along the line it became clear to me that this can't possibly work. And there is no way that the changes that would need to be made would ever be allowed. But I couldn't change! I was the poster child for the cause! I had to keep it going!"

In contrast the people I know who grow and live in a supple way are cautious about their commitments. Not that they don't make them, but they are judicious and realize how tentative those roles and activities are.

What are the anchors in your life? What are the things which tie you down and prevent you from changing and growing? What are the things you might lose if you changed? What would it be like to emotionally streamline your life and have fewer anchors, fewer things that define you and limit you?

5. Discipline and deliberateness

This isn't the same thing as rigidity. It means the practice of doing things on purpose, deliberately, and the discipline to follow through on those decisions. Yoga, for example, is a discipline designed to give a person the ability to make decisions about their body and behavior and just do it.

A few years ago I casually tossed out an assignment for a client, which sounded innocent enough. He was feeling out of control and I suggested that for the next week he should go ahead and do whatever he did, but to take a Moment to consciously decide to do it, and do it on purpose. For example if he scratched his nose, he was to *decide* to scratch his nose. If he stood up, he was to *decide* to stand up.

Sounds easy, right?

Wrong.

He called me a few minutes later from the parking lot and said that it was hard to do it for even a few minutes. I tried it and I agreed. To consciously decide each word that you say, each movement that you make, is rewarding but difficult. In our society we are rewarded for thinking that we are just responding to external stimuli, that our thoughts and feelings and actions are dictated by circumstances and we have few choices. Essentially, this says that our lives are not our own and we have no control over our lives or ourselves.

The calm people I know or am aware of, the Un-Stuck people, do not attribute their thoughts and feelings and actions externally. They do not take the position that they are out of control of their lives or actions. Instead they make a point of being conscious of the decisions they make, that they are deciding to do what they do. Because it's part of their lifestyle it isn't that hard for them to do.

They make a point of deciding. They make a practice of not doing things automatically or casually or thoughtlessly.

Being stuck is the perfect example of the **opposite** of doing things deliberately. It's doing the same things automatically, without thinking. It's doing things because we feel externally controlled, constrained.

Kevin's life was out of control. He was trying to lead an adult life with the coping skills of a teenager. An avoider. He was behind on everything, taxes, bills, his unfinished divorce, various legal problems, work problems, the list was endless. He lived crisis to crisis. He never opened his mail or answered his phone. He was miserable.

By maximizing his discomfort with the crisis living and by maximizing his desire to have one part of his life in order, we agreed on a plan that he would sort out all of his mail into three piles; bills to pay, problems to solve, and garbage.

Once he threw out the garbage he was left with bills and problems to solve. He focused on the bills. He sorted them out in rank order of the smallest bill to the biggest.

The smallest bill was an insignificant amount, so he paid it. The next week he paid the next biggest bill and so forth.

One step at a time he became a more disciplined, deliberate person. He always opened his mail and paid each bill on time the day it arrived. He always answered his phone and gave each problem his full, undivided attention until it was solved.

He didn't stop when the immediate problem was solved. He became a disciplined, deliberate person. His life became happier, freer, Un-Stuck. He lived on purpose. By choice.

In order to live Un-Stuck, cultivate the sense of deliberateness, of discipline. And not just a sense, the **practice** of living deliberately, consciously. [6]

---

[6] William Glasser, *Control Theory* is a wonderful source of ideas on this subject.

- Decide what you are going to do and do it. Every time you find yourself doing things randomly, catch yourself, pause, and decide to do them.
- Make realistic plans and do them. Practice doing it. Start with something simple and work your way up until making plans and doing them becomes a part of your life.
- If you catch yourself attributing your actions to external forces or chance, catch yourself and go back to thinking responsibly;
    - Instead of thinking "I just did it" say "I chose to do it".
    - Instead of telling yourself "I had no choice" tell yourself "I made a choice".
    - Instead of believing "I didn't do anything" believe "I made a decision to do nothing."

Everything we do, think or feel is purposeful and only when we admit to ourselves that we do, think or feel those things for a purpose can we realize what that purpose is and take charge of that purpose and never be emotionally trapped again, never be stuck again.

CONCLUSION:

Welcome to the beginning!

You've come a long way. You started to read this book because you felt trapped, stuck, and wanted freedom from the prison of your identity. An out-of-date identity which limited you and left you unable to live the life you needed to live today.

You have learned that what we call an identity is not who we are, but merely the collection of ideas and beliefs and skills we use to get by, which needs to be updated periodically.

You have learned that you can update this paradigm as needed so that you can adapt and mature and grow fluidly and joyfully.

And now you can put it to work. You can begin to actively question the limitations in your life, actively question the assumption which limited you, and actively work to expand your life and your identity and your joy.

And now you can continue your personal evolution into the person you were meant to be. You can allow yourself to change and evolve into the person you want, like having shoes the right size.

You can make this fluidity and suppleness and adaptability a way of life that you can continue as long as you live, always seeking out new ideas and experiences which fulfill you.

Thank you for allowing me and this book to be part of that adventure.

ABOUT THE AUTHOR

Doug Bartholomew, MS, LMHC, was born and raised in Washington and has worked in the mental health field in the Puget Sound area since 1975. He has been in private practice in Bellevue, Washington since 1990.

He received his Bachelor's degree in psychology from Whitman College in Walla Walla, Washington and his Master of Science degree in psychology from Western Washington University in Bellingham, Washington. He has completed the training for the Gottman Method of marital therapy and he is certified in Heart Centered Hypnotherapy from the Wellness Institute in Issaquah, Washington.

His website is www.doug-bartholomew.com

ABOUT THE EVOLUTION-DIRECTED THERAPY SERIES

This is the first book from the EVOLUTION-DIRECTED THERAPY series to be published. The other books, to come out soon, include;

- Evolution-Directed Therapy
- Searching Your Soul: A Guide to Looking in the Right Places
- The Seven Struggles of the Troubled Heart
- The Art of Feeling Bad Correctly
- The Nemesis Effect; On Hate, Hating and Being Hated

Made in the USA
Charleston, SC
04 August 2016